THE
LORD'S PRAYER
in Its Biblical Setting

THE
LORD'S PRAYER
in Its Biblical Setting

CHARLES M. LAYMON

ABINGDON PRESS
NASHVILLE AND NEW YORK

THE LORD'S PRAYER IN ITS BIBLICAL SETTING

Copyright © 1968 by Abingdon Press

Library of Congress Catalog Card Number: 68-25362

Scripture quotations unless otherwise noted are from the
Revised Standard Version of the Bible, copyrighted 1946
and 1952 by the Division of Christian Education, National Council of Churches, and are used by permission.

Quotations from *The Dead Sea Scriptures* by Theodor
H. Gaster. Copyright © 1956, 1964 by Theodor H. Gaster.
Reprinted by permission of Doubleday & Company, Inc.

To My Wife, Virginia

*whose sensitivity to spiritual
truth has been an inspiration
in the writing of this book*

Contents

Prologue

The place of the Lord's Prayer in the life of the church, both in its corporate worship and in the individual devotional practices of its members, has been marked. From the Gospels no passage has found greater use unless it be the words of the institution of the Lord's Supper, first recorded, however, not in one of the Gospels, but in Paul's First Epistle to the Corinthians (11: 23-26).

Reasons for Its Extensive Use

The reasons for the extensive use of the Lord's Prayer are at least threefold. First of all it is Jesus' prayer; its

9

origin goes back to him. Whatever sentiments it may share with the prayers of the Old Testament and Judaism, it remains his very own, both in its origin and individual character. This fact commends the prayer to all who follow him.

In the second place, the Lord's Prayer has become the prayer of the church itself. No other prayer of Jesus or of his times was taken into the worship and liturgy of the Christian community as was this one. Although we know little in detail about the earliest Christian liturgy, the second-century *Didache*, which was the first of a type of writing known as "Church Orders" and probably contains some materials going back to apostolic times, told Christians to pray the Lord's Prayer three times daily. It was taught to the catechumens when they were baptized. Cyprian in the third century A.D. referred to it as both a public and common prayer.

In the third place, the Lord's Prayer speaks to man's innermost spiritual longings. Here is where he lives—or would live—as a child of God. His desire to praise God, his need to look to him for daily sustenance, his conviction that there is an active Divine Being at work in the world as he expresses his will on earth, and his longing for forgiveness and support as he seeks to meet the moral demand for righteousness—all these and more he finds in the Lord's Prayer. As Archbishop William Temple said: "It is the prayer you would want to offer if you loved God with all your heart."[1]

[1] William Temple, *Christian Faith and Life* (London: SCM Press, 1957), p. 111.

Early Commentaries

The fact that early patristic commentaries presented interpretations of the Lord's Prayer is yet another indication of the serious attention the church gave to it from the beginning. Some of these include the works of Tertullian (c. 160-220), *De Oratione,* XXII-XXX, Cyprian (c. 200-258), *De Dominica Oratione,* and Augustine (354-430), *De Sermone Domini in Monte,* 11, 15-39.[2]

From these distant days on, commentary on the Lord's Prayer has come from church leaders such as the mystic Meister Eckhart (c. 1260-1327), Thomas Aquinas (c. 1225-1274), Martin Luther (1483-1546), and John Wesley (1703-1791). Tertullian referred to it as "the epitome of the whole gospel." Luther said, "The Lord's Prayer is the highest, noblest, and best prayer; all other prayers shall be suspected which do not have or contain the content and meaning of this prayer."

A Principle of Interpretation

The Lord's Prayer needs to be interpreted if it is to be not only understood but also prayed. The familiar invitation to "repeat the Lord's Prayer" more often than not keeps us from entering into its meaning. It is not simply an item on a liturgical order of service; rather, it is a prayer and a proclamation of Christian beliefs. The

[2] Cf. F. H. Chase, *The Lord's Prayer in the Early Church.* Texts and Studies, I.3 (Cambridge, 1891).

religion of the Lord's Prayer is one with the essence of the teachings of Jesus.

The brief statements of the prayer must therefore be read in the light of our Lord's teaching as a whole concerning God, the Kingdom, providence, forgiveness, and the Father's deliverance from evil. Jesus' total teaching and ministry undergird it. To abstract it from this historical soil is to substitute artificial flowers for living blossoms. The meanings of its petitions do not come to us out of thin air, but only after a careful study of the religious heritage from which it came, of both the Hebrew and Christian traditions.

The approach in this book seeks to take into consideration the total biblical background of the Lord's Prayer, including the setting of both the Old and New Testaments. It also takes account of the prayer life at the synagogue as far as this can be ascertained, recognizing that this institution was a school more than a center for worship.[3]

Since the covenanters of the Dead Sea Scroll community at Qumran represent an authentic Hebrew tradition, some note has been taken of their prayer life also. No attempt was made to suggest a borrowing-source relationship where the Lord's Prayer was concerned. This would be difficult to establish at best. The broader impact of the spiritual outlook and practices of the Essenes

[3] A helpful study on Hebraic backgrounds of the Lord's Prayer is found in Israel Abrahams, *Studies in Pharisaism and the Gospels* (New York: Cambridge University Press, 1924), Ch. XII. Cf. also Gustaf H. Dalman, *The Words of Jesus* (Edinburgh: T. and T. Clark, 1902), pp. 283-365.

is of more significance here than the drawing of exact parallels. Israel Abrahams' observation is particularly sound at this point: "Composed under the inspiration of Hebraic ideas, modelled to a large extent on Jewish forms, it [the Lord's Prayer] was not in its primitive form a mosaic but a whole and fresh design." [4] It was Jesus who contributed the "whole and fresh design."

A cursory reading of the table of contents might suggest that a treatment of some of the petitions of the Lord's Prayer is missing—where are the customary seven? The explanation is found within the book. It is sufficient to note here that the petition to hallow God's name is considered the culmination of the opening address. The petition for God's will to be done on earth as in heaven is regarded as a poetic parallelism that defines the meaning of "Thy kingdom come." And finally the prayer for deliverance from evil is viewed as belonging in this same sense to the petition "Lead us not into temptation."

Most of the books written on the Lord's Prayer are devotional in character. This is understandable in view of our customary use of this prayer. The present volume takes its stance from the conviction that the life of the spirit can rise no higher than the roots of understanding will allow; at least this is the place to begin. The studied explanation of the meaning of a word or phrase in the light of its historical background is no less a spiritual concern than instruction in prayer procedures or devotional exhortations.

[4] *Studies in Pharisaism and the Gospels,* p. 100.

This book has been written for thoughtful Christians, both professional and lay, who, through a sounder knowledge of the religion they profess, would enter more deeply into its spiritual treasures through a fuller understanding of the Lord's Prayer.

Chapter I

Prayer in the Old Testament

The Hebrews were a praying people. Because it is found within the stream of Judaic-Christian revelation, the Lord's Prayer must be understood in the light of this fact. We see in the Old Testament that their earliest heroes prayed to God as naturally as sparks fly heavenward. Prayer was not argued but practiced. No one questioned praying; to inquire whether it were valid or beneficial did not seem to have occurred to them.

They were like the Arab who said to Lawrence of Arabia: "You foreigners see millions of stars and nothing beyond. We Arabs see only a few stars—*and God.*" It was because God was real to them that prayer was real also. The two go together.

The Patriarchs Prayed

In the biblical narratives of Genesis we find numerous illustrations of the prayer life of the patriarchs. These worthies of the past prayed in connection with the issues that affected their lives most deeply. It was when the meaning of existence was at stake, their nation's in particular, that they prayed most.

Abraham, for instance, prayed that through his son Ishmael the promise of God to the patriarch, that he would be the father of a great nation, would be fulfilled (Gen. 17:18).[1] Any other possibility seemed hopeless. His wife Sarah was too aged to bear children. How else could the promise be fulfilled? And even though God had told Abraham that Sarah would conceive and give birth to a son, Abraham had laughed at the idea (Gen. 17:17). Ishmael was here, a living fact. Let him be the one.

Prayer on this occasion brought to Abraham the realization that the obvious is not always God's way. The as yet unseen may contain God's providential purpose more than what is there before one's eyes. Abraham was told that the unborn son of Sarah would be the one through whom the promise would be fulfilled. His prayer in one

---

[1] This is one of the priestly narratives, so called because they were transmitted by the priestly group in Israel and are usually dated around 500 B.C.

sense was unanswered; yet in another, it was more than answered.

On a later occasion, Abraham prayed when the lives of his kinsmen Lot and Lot's family were at stake (Gen. 18:22-33).[2] In true oriental fashion he offered a prayer that is unique among the recorded prayers of the Old Testament. Step by step, the patriarch asked his petitions. Each time he received an affirmative reply he increased his askings, almost as though he were bargaining with God.

Would God spare wicked Sodom where Lot and his family dwelt if there were fifty righteous persons living there; then forty-five, then forty, twenty, and finally ten? The last figure was sufficient to cover Lot and his kinsmen. When Abraham was assured that if there were ten righteous in Sodom, God would not destroy the city, he ceased his praying and with dignity went his way.

This prayer in which the fate of others was the chief concern is a moving example of intercessory praying. It is all the more remarkable coming from the ancient past and reflects the outlook of a day in which the group—in this case Abraham's family—was regarded as more important than the individual.

Among the records of the prayer experiences of the patriarchs of Israel none is more impressive than the account of Jacob's wrestling with the angel (Gen. 32:22-

[2] This is a story that was remembered and recorded in southern Palestine. It belongs to the J group of narratives which use the name *Jahweh* for God and are dated around 950 B.C.

31).[3] Filled with symbolism the narrative tells how he struggled all night with God's messenger, refusing to let him go until he had blessed him.

Jacob's uncertain past was catching up with him. He had tricked his brother Esau, deceived his father Isaac, run away under questionable circumstances from his uncle Laban—and now he was facing God before he would have to meet Esau who was moving in his direction.

At the time of his vision at Bethel in which he saw a ladder reaching from earth to heaven (Gen. 28:10 ff.), Jacob had been told that the promise made with Abraham would be fulfilled through him (vss. 13-15). But his life had been far from exemplary, and now in his confrontation with God, which was essentially a prayer experience, Jacob was making peace with God.

The significant element in this prayer experience was Jacob's seriousness and persistence. These prefigure Jesus' prayer parables of the Importunate Widow (Luke 18:1-8), and the Friend at Midnight (Luke 11:5-8) where his followers were urged to keep knocking at the door of heaven in prayer (cf. also Matt. 7:7-12). God will assuredly answer.

Moses Prayed

Moses is not counted among the patriarchs of Israel, but he belongs with these leaders in the nation's past

---

[3] This is a J account. Cf. footnote #2.

whose lives influenced its destiny and for whom prayer was most real. Among the records of Moses at prayer is found a moving account of his defense of his people before God. They had sinned, rebelled, were a stiff-necked group, and God was deciding to destroy them. Because of this, in an anthropomorphic fashion, God said to Moses who was interceding on their behalf: "Now therefore let me alone, that my wrath may burn hot against them and I may consume them" (Exod. 32:10).[4]

But Moses held on to his purpose, arguing that God would appear ridiculous in the eyes of the Egyptians if he destroyed his people (Exod. 32:12). Besides this, Moses asked whether God did not intend to carry out his promises to Abraham, Isaac, and Jacob (Israel) that he would bring into being through them a great people (Exod. 32:13).

Moses' prayer on this occasion reached its greatest height when he volunteered to be destroyed himself, now and forever, if only the people would be forgiven and spared destruction: "If thou wilt forgive their sin—and if not, blot me, I pray thee, out of thy book which thou hast written" (Exod. 32:32). Again one is reminded of the New Testament portrait of Jesus as one who died for the sins of others on a cross.

One more prayer of Moses needs to be mentioned. It all but reaches a New Testament level in its petition for the continued and lively presence of God. Moses was about,

[4] This is one of the narratives coming from northern Palestine. They are known as the E accounts and use the name *Elohim* for God.

as he thought, to take the people into the Promised Land, back to Palestine. He saw, however, that it would not be the eldorado of their dreams unless God himself accompanied them.

In the words of the Lord's Prayer which we shall later consider, how could God's will be done on earth if God were not with them? Moses was convinced that even the wilderness where God had given the Law and providentially cared for the people by sending manna and providing water—even this terrifying wilderness with God present in their midst was to be preferred above Palestine with God absent. And so he prayed: "If thy presence will not go with me, do not carry us up from here. . . . Is it not in thy going with us, so that we are distinct, I and thy people, from all other people that are upon the face of the earth?" (Exod. 33:15-16.) [5]

This prayer of Moses shows that the Hebrews had not yet fully realized the fact of God's universal presence. It was almost as though unless he "traveled" with them they were deprived of his nearness. The prayer also indicates that the Hebrews were taking seriously the fact that they were a "distinct" people, the people with whom God had made a covenant.

The Kings Prayed

The kings of the Hebrews were varied in character and effectiveness. Some like David, Uzziah, and Josiah were

---

[5] This is a J account. Cf. footnote #2.

crowned with nobility as well as political authority. Others such as Ahab and Manasseh were evil and weak in character. The biblical understanding of political rule, however, continued to be kept alive through the centuries in spite of lapses and tragic departures.

This biblical ideal was that of a theocracy. The king ruled, to be sure, but he did so under God. He was responsible to him for what he did as he governed the people of God. The account of how the Hebrews came to have their first king, Saul, is revealing in this respect (I Sam. 9:1–10:16). He was anointed by the prophet to rule, having been pointed out to Samuel by God himself.[6]

Sometimes the kings forgot this responsibility to be God's servants and the prophets had to remind them of this fact. Power wrongly understood and used corrupted in those days even as it does today.

Rulers pray just as other men, and the Hebrew kings were no exception. Some of their prayers were recorded by the biblical writers. They prayed in varied situations and for different purposes. For instance, David prayed that the people should not suffer because he had sinned in taking a census (II Sam. 24:17). He offered a prayer of thanksgiving for the willingness of the people to give offerings toward the building of the Temple (I Chron. 29:10 ff.). And he also prayed when told that, although

[6] There is another story here that suggests that God unwillingly gave his people a king, acquiescing only because of their urging (I Sam. 8:4-22; 10:17-27).

21

he could not build the Temple, his throne would be established forever (II Sam. 7:13b ff.).

The words of David's prayer on this occasion were recorded by the biblical author as being both noteworthy and ideal:

Who am I, O Lord God, and what is my house, that thou hast brought me thus far? And yet this was a small thing in thy eyes, O Lord God; thou hast spoken also of thy servant's house for a great while to come, and hast shown me future generations, O Lord God! (II Sam. 7:18b-19.)

Perhaps the most remembered prayer of all the kings of the Hebrews was Solomon's petition for wisdom and understanding when he undertook his responsibilities as king. Told to ask for whatever he wished, he prayed:

O Lord my God, thou hast made thy servant king in place of David my father, although I am but a little child; I do not know how to go out or come in. And thy servant is in the midst of thy people whom thou hast chosen, a great people, that cannot be numbered or counted for multitude. Give thy servant therefore an understanding mind to govern thy people, that I may discern between good and evil; for who is able to govern this thy great people? (I Kings 3: 7-9.)

Solomon was unable under the pressures of government to live up to his prayer for understanding. Although he gained a reputation for wisdom, he placed such burdens upon his people that at his death his kingdom fell apart. From then on we have the northern kingdom known as Israel, and the southern called Judah.[7]

The Prophets Prayed

The prophets were the most unique of all the Old Testament personalities. They made a contribution to the religion of the Hebrews that was unmatched. As the interpreters of God's will for his people in the day in which they lived, they were in such close union with him that their words were his WORD and their thoughts his thoughts. They could say, "Thus says the Lord," and it was true.

Such men as this could be expected to be praying men. Their closeness to God made their daily lives a constant prayer, whether they verbalized their longings and desires or not. Sometimes their prayers were centered in their work among the people; at other times their personal experiences veritably drew prayers out of them.

Take, for instance, the prayer of Elijah on Mount Carmel where a contest was staged to decide who was the true Divine Being, God or Baal. There were many baals since this worship was polytheistic, each field or area having its local deity. The Hebrews were adding to their own religious observances immoral practices from baal worship which was a fertility cult. Hence the challenge of Elijah the prophet: "How long will you go limping

[7] Another of Solomon's notable prayers that was recorded is the one which he offered when the Temple was dedicated and he saw it as a place of prayer (I Kings 8:23-53).

with two different opinions? If the Lord is God, follow him; but if Baal, then follow him" (I Kings 18:21).

The account of the contest relates the dramatic activities of the priests of Baal as they prayed to their god to send down fire and consume their offering on the altar. In contrast Elijah made a simple prayer in the vein of Jesus' word that men are not heard for much speaking: "Answer me, O Lord, answer me, that this people may know that thou, O Lord, art God" (I Kings 18:37). The fire fell.

Elisha once prayed a memorable prayer. It too was brief, but the purpose behind it adds to its magnitude. His servant was in a frenzy of fear because of the threat of the Syrian army against Israel. The town of Dothan where they were staying had been surrounded, and destruction seemed inevitable. The servant cried out: "Alas my master! What shall we do?"

Do? Elisha prayed a most simple prayer: "O Lord, I pray thee, open his eyes that he may see" (II Kings 6:17). Whereupon the youth's eyes were opened and he saw that the mountains round about were full of horses and chariots of fire. This was the invisible army of the Lord that was ever present to help. It had been there all the time; prayer had brought an awareness of the divine presence.

Sometimes the prophets prayed for themselves in their hours of need. Jeremiah did this so frequently that he has become known as the father of personal religion in the Old Testament. Perhaps no prophet of the Hebrew people suffered as much as Jeremiah. Both the nature of the times and his own sensitivity contributed to this fact. He was frequently persecuted, insulted, and defamed throughout a ministry that lasted forty years.

On one occasion Jeremiah prayed:

> O Lord, thou knowest;
> > remember me and visit me,
> > and take vengeance for me on my
> > > persecutors.
> In thy forbearance take me not
> > away;
> > know that for thy sake I bear
> > reproach.
> Thy words were found, and I ate
> > them,
> > and thy words became to me a
> > joy
> > and the delight of my heart.
> > > (Jer. 15:15-16.)

Then he added:

> I sat alone, because thy hand was
> > upon me,
> > for thou hadst filled me with
> > indignation.
> Why is my pain unceasing,
> my wound incurable,
> refusing to be healed? (15:17b-18a.)

Like Jesus who later on a cross of suffering cried out "Why?" so Jeremiah put his question to God. Like

Jesus also who wept for Jerusalem, Jeremiah exclaimed: "O that my head were waters, and my eyes a fountain of tears, that I might weep day and night for the slain of the daughter of my people!" (9:1.)

Prayer for the prophets was intensely personal. How could it have been otherwise for these men who were "called" to prophesy? Conversation with God was the natural language in such a relationship.

The Psalmists Prayed

In the Old Testament prayer reached its highest level with the psalmists. As a collection of the poetry of the Hebrew people the Psalter abounds in great thrusts of the human spirit heavenward. Many of these contain prayers that have provided wings for the thoughts and longings of mankind in the Judaic-Christian tradition through the centuries.

There is an unstudied spontaneity in these prayers that mark them as truly religious. Whenever prayer becomes formal and self-consciously devotional, it turns out to be merely a collection of words.

In many psalms the psalmist will begin by speaking of his situation or by addressing himself to others. As his sense of God's presence deepens, however, he begins to pray without even realizing that he has changed the object of his address. Take the familiar twenty-third psalm. The author opens by extolling the providential care of the Lord as his shepherd. Not only in life but also in death does this concern for him persist.

When he refers to death, however, the author, having said that he will fear no evil, turns directly to God and begins to pray:

> for *thou* art with me;
>   *thy* rod and thy staff,
>   they comfort me.
>
> *Thou* preparest a table before me
>   in the presence of my enemies;
> *thou* anointest my head with oil,
>   my cup overflows. (Ps. 23:4*b*-5.)

At this point the psalmist turns once again to the people and reasserts his faith that goodness and mercy shall be his as long as he lives, and that he will dwell in the Lord's house forever.

Sometimes the psalms begin with a cry to God, a cry out of deepest desperation. Psalm twenty-two is of this character:

> My God, my God, why hast
>   thou forsaken me?
>
> Why art thou so far from
>   helping me, from the
>   words of my groaning?

Because of this surge of intimacy in despair, Jesus could utter these same words from the cross as his pain became unbearable.

For the psalmists praise is an important part of praying, as in the case of psalm eight:

> O Lord, our Lord,
> how majestic is thy name in all the earth! (Ps. 8:1.)

Here is another:

> I love thee, O Lord, my strength. (Ps. 18:1.)

Then the writer moves on to tell others why he loves God. He is worthy to be praised and has saved him from his enemies (vs. 3). When threatened with death the Lord delivered him (vss. 4-6). Ah, he asks,

> Who is God, but the Lord?
> And who is a rock, except our God? (Vs. 31.)

The various subjects about which the psalmists pray are multiple. In addition to those already mentioned, he sometimes shares with God his appreciation of the Temple, saying:

> How lovely is thy dwelling place,
> O Lord of hosts! (Ps. 84:1.)

Again, he gives thanks for the law of God that he finds within his heart. In almost a New Testament vein he prays:

> I delight to do thy will, O my God;
>   thy law is within my heart. (Ps. 40:8.)

Illustrations of this kind of praying by the psalmists could be multiplied many times over. These are sufficient to show how deeply personal are their prayers. There is nothing perfunctory or artificial here. Spirit is meeting spirit on the deepest of all possible levels of communication. This is true prayer.

Prayers of the Dead Sea Community

The writings of the Essenes who lived in the Dead Sea community at Qumran (c. 170 B.C.–A.D. 68) are not found in the Old Testament but also represent a particular line of Hebraic religious culture that is authentic. Among these is a collection of hymns and psalms which reflect the prayer spirit and attitude of these covenanters.

It is not possible to date many, if any, of them specifically so that the exact background of the reference involved in a prayer passage cannot be stated. Several of them are pertinent to this consideration of the Hebrew prayers of the Old Testament.[8]

Believing that they were the true covenant people of God, this group was capable of reaching worthy heights of religious sensitivity. Their hymns and prayers reflect this. For instance, the "Hymn of the Initiants" (Manual

---

[8] The translations used are those of Theodor H. Gaster in *The Dead Sea Scriptures* (Garden City, N.Y.: Doubleday, 1956).

of Discipline, cols. X-XI) closes with what is essentially a prayer of praise:

> Blessed art Thou, O my God,
> Who hast opened the heart of Thy servant unto
>   knowledge.
> Direct all his works in righteousness,
> and vouchsafe unto the son of Thine handmaid
> the favor which Thou hast assured to all the mortal
>   elect,
> to stand in Thy presence for ever.
>   For apart from Thee no man's way can be perfect,
> and without Thy will is nothing wrought. . . .
> Who can compass the sum of Thy glory?
> And what is mere mortal man
> amid Thy wondrous works?
> And what the child of woman
> to sit in Thy presence?

Various themes of praise are found in the "Book of Hymns" as prayer is lifted to God. Note some of the following:

> [Thou art the source of all might]
> and the wellspring of all power;
> [yet art Thou also rich in wisdom]
>   [and] great in counsel. (From I, 5-39.)

> I give thanks unto Thee, O Lord,
> for Thine eye is ever awake,
> watching over my soul. (From II, 31-36.)

30

[I give thanks unto Thee, O Lord,]
for Thou hast illumined [my face]
[with the vision of Thy truth;]
wherefore I yet shall walk in glory everlasting
along with all [the holy that hear the words
   of] thy mouth,
and Thou wilt deliver me from [the pit and
   the slough.] (From III, 3-18.)

I give thanks unto Thee, O Lord,
for Thou hast been unto me a strong wall
against all that would destroy me
and all that would [traduce me.]
   Thou dost shelter me from the disasters
of a turbulant time, [   ]
that it come not. [   ] (From III, 37-IV, 4.)

Other selections could be cited, but these prayers are sufficient to show that there is a continuity of devotion and faith between the psalmists of the Old Testament Psalter and the saints of the Dead Sea community. All prayed for knowledge and wisdom, protection in time of danger, and for vision and illumination.

The prayers of the Old Testament, whether those of the patriarchs, kings, prophets, or psalmists, reveal a deep devotional life and exhibit faith and trust in God among the vicissitudes of existence. The Lord's Prayer belongs within the context of this same living relationship to God. It cannot be considered as a statement apart from the religion of the people to whom God had first given the Covenant, and to whom he had sent the Son.

31

Chapter II

Prayer and the Synagogue

In any study of the prayers of Jesus the religious services of the synagogue should be considered, because Jesus matured within the influence of the synagogue and continued to attend it in adulthood. The Gospel of Luke's account of Jesus' visit to the Nazareth synagogue reads: "And he came to Nazareth, where he had been brought up; and he went to the synagogue, *as his custom was,* on the sabbath day" (4:16). He probably attended school there as a boy and worshiped there as a man.

Would it be too much to say that Jesus learned to pray the prayers of the Jewish fathers mostly at the synagogue,

32

because these were offered there as a part of its program?
He also became acquainted there with the religious traditions of his people, and their practice of prayer was a part
of these traditions. Just as most present-day Christians
who are reared in the church have their conception and
practice of prayer influenced by this fact, Jesus' thought
of prayer and his own prayer life must have been affected
by the synagogue. This would not negate his uniqueness
or personal touch in prayer, but it does relate his own
prayers and praying to this institution. Since Jesus' con-
tacts with the Temple were few, his frequent associations
with the synagogue must have influenced him most.

The Origin of the Synagogue

By the time Jesus was born the synagogue was an
established institution within Judaism. It had not always
had a building and other external trappings which it
possessed in Jesus' day; these came with its growth and
development. Neither had it been as widespread in days
gone by, but in the first century A.D. nearly every town or
city had its own. This made the spread and continuation
of Judaism possible throughout the Greco-Roman world
and also provided a base for preaching for the first Christian missionaries. More than this, it is likely that the
earliest Christian worship was fashioned after the forms
used in the synagogue.[1] At the outset, most of the first

[1] George Foote Moore, *Judaism in the First Centuries of the
Christian Era* (Cambridge: Harvard University Press, 1930),
I, 285.

Christians were converts from Judaism who would bring with them into the Christian community their inherited and familiar practices from the synagogue.

Although traditionally ascribed to Moses, the exact origin of the synagogue is unknown. A probable beginning may be found in the gathering of the elders at the home of Ezekiel in Babylon.[2] Jerusalem was in ruins; the Temple with its sacrifices had been burned; the Hebrews were hundreds of miles away from their homeland. Drawing together for remembrance, instruction, prayer, and praise would meet their desperate need for religious association and fellowship.

Even after the Temple had been rebuilt and its sacrifices were once more being offered, the need for this coming together of the faithful remained. Its value had been discovered to be too great to be dismissed. Not only in Babylon, but wherever Jews were deprived of the Temple services the synagogue would meet a deep religious need. In time, even in Jerusalem where the Temple stood synagogues sprang up, suggesting that here was a form of service that had made a place for itself apart from the Temple, so that it "belonged" to official Judaism.

The intermediary stages by which the synagogue reached this position are not clearly marked either within or outside the Scriptures. Possibly the reference in psalm 149:1 to "the assembly of the faithful" refers to the

[2] Cf. Ezek. 8:1; 14:1; 20:1.

34

synagogue, and perhaps the mention of "the congregation of the righteous" in psalm 1:5 does also.

When we find it functioning in Jesus' time, the Pharisees are clearly making great use of it. This group which probably goes back to the Hasidim in the days of the Maccabean struggle found in the synagogue an opportunity for instruction in the beliefs and practices of Judaism. What better way to equip the people to hold fast to the tradition of the fathers when men of violence were about to destroy their worship? Although they did not originate it, the Pharisees made prime use of the synagogue.

The Synagogue as a School

Religious education was one, if not the main, function of the synagogue. Here the Law was read and interpreted; here the Jews learned of their past history; here the first translation of the Pentateuch into Greek was probably used abroad by Greek-speaking Jews.

Philo, the Hellenistic Jewish philosopher, regarded the synagogue much in the same light as the schools of philosophy in his day.[3] Hebrew philosophy, he believed, was being taught there just as the philosophies of Socrates, Plato, and Aristotle were expounded elsewhere.

We may assume that Jesus was able to refer to the Old Testament so frequently because of the teaching he had received at the synagogue. The chances against his

[3] Cf. *Vita Mosis*, iii, 27 π 211.

35

owning Old Testament scrolls are marked. And although his own home was undoubtedly pious in the Hebrew sense of true piety, such detailed knowledge of the traditions of his people would not likely have come from family instruction.

Had the synagogue provided no other service than to instruct Jesus in the issues, personalities, and history of his nation's past, it would have served more than a noble purpose and justified its existence. Without it, Jesus might not have been *the Jesus of history* as we know him.

Worship in the Synagogue

In addition to the instructional purposes of the synagogue there was its significance as a house of worship. Here was the people's service, their share in the cult. It has been suggested that the knowledge of the prophets awakened the people to realize that they too could approach God. The priest was not the only person who could claim access to the divine throne. More than this, there were other ways of praying besides the offerings and sacrifices of the Temple.[4]

There was a tendency, however, for the synagogue to carry over into its services some elements from the Tem-

[4] Cf. A. Z. Idelsohn, *Jewish Liturgy and Its Development* (New York: Henry Holt, 1932), p. 24. F. C. Grant, however, places the study of God's word above the worship; cf. *Ancient Judaism and the New Testament* (New York: The Macmillan Co., 1959).

ple. Certain phrases used in the Temple prayers found their way into the synagogue. This would be inevitable, particularly with the Temple in ruins. Even with it intact, however, there was some similarity in this regard, although the sacrifices and offerings and priestly cult were missing in the synagogue itself.

Prayer was offered in the synagogue three times daily, a custom perhaps grown out of a reference to Daniel who "got down upon his knees three times a day and prayed and gave thanks before his God" (Dan. 6:10).[5] Another explanation offered referred to the legend that the three patriarchs prayed—Abraham in the morning (Gen. 19:27), Isaac at eventide (Gen. 24:63), and Jacob at night (Gen. 28:11). Those who could not come to the synagogue for the three services each day were urged to pray elsewhere, in the field, in the house, or even while lying in bed.

The Shema

The prayers of the synagogue were preceded by a recitation of the *Shema*, the confession of faith in the unity of God, found in Deuteronomy 6:4: "Hear, O Israel: The Lord our God is one Lord; and you shall love the Lord your God with all your heart, and with all your soul, and with all your might." Jesus combined this with Leviticus 19:18: "You shall love your neighbor as your-

---

[5] Cf. also psalm 55:17: "Evening and morning and at noon I utter my complaint and moan, and he will hear my voice."

self," to comprise what we call the Great Commandment (Mark 12:29-31).

In affirming the unity of God before offering the petitions, or the Tefillah, which followed, the character of the God to whom prayer was to be offered was defined. Thus the true setting for the prayers was established. This is not unlike what Jesus did in the opening section of the Lord's Prayer where the "address" precedes the separate petitions. When this is done, prayer occurs within focus of the final truth about God. It affects the character of all that is said afterward. Nothing in the practice of prayer is more basic than this.

The Eighteen Benedictions

After the Shema was recited a series of eighteen benedictions followed. They are referred to as Benedictions, sometimes as Blessings, because at the close of each there is a response beginning with the words: "Blessed art thou, O Lord." [6] There are really nineteen, but since an early arrangement toward the close of the first century made at Jamnia under the direction of Rabbi Gamaliel (II) contained but eighteen, this title remained even though an additional one was added. They are called the Shemoneh 'Esreh, and appear in that part of the synagogue service known as the Tefillah.

The Eighteen Benedictions were regarded as being

[6] Cf. the article "Amidah" in *The Encyclopedia of the Jewish Religion,* ed. Werblowsky and Wigoder (New York: Holt, Rinehart and Winston, 1966), pp. 27-28.

composed by the Great Synagogue. This was a somewhat legendary council made up of the great men of Israel, its origin going back to the time of Ezra and Nehemiah who were credited with authority for making ordinances and regulations for Judaism. It has been suggested that the term Assembly or Convention would be preferable.

The Benedictions when carefully examined show a close affiliation with the psalms. Their phrasing and spirit are psalmodic. Since the book of Psalms was the hymnal, so to speak, of the second temple, it is likely that the temple ritual itself influenced the Benedictions. The prayers of individual persons may also have been incorporated among the eighteen. Some find the doctrines of the Pharisees reflected in certain of the statements, particularly in the second benediction which refers to the resurrection of the dead.

Following are the Eighteen Benedictions:

I. Blessed art thou, O Lord our God and God of our fathers, God of Abraham, God of Isaac, and God of Jacob, the great, mighty and revered God, the most high God, who bestowest lovingkindnesses, and possessest all things; who rememberest the pious deeds of the patriarchs, and in love wilt bring a redeemer to their children's children for thy name's sake. O King, Helper, Saviour and Shield. Blessed art thou, O Lord, the Shield of Abraham.

II. Thou, O Lord, art mighty for ever, thou quickenest the dead, thou art mighty to save. Thou sustainest the living with lovingkindness, quickenest the dead with great mercy, supportest the falling, healest the sick, loosest the bound, and keepest thy faith to them that sleep in the dust. Who is like unto thee, Lord of mighty acts, and who resembleth thee, O King, who killest and quickenest, and causest salvation to spring forth? Yea, faithful art thou to quicken the dead. Blessed art thou, O Lord, who quickenest the dead.

III. Thou art holy, and thy name is holy, and holy beings praise thee daily. (Selah) Blessed art thou, O Lord, the holy God.

IV. Thou favourest man with knowledge, and teachest mortals understanding. O favour us with knowledge, understanding and discernment from thee. Blessed art thou, O Lord, gracious Giver of knowledge.

V. Cause us to return, O our Father, unto thy Law; draw us near, O our King, unto thy service, and bring us back in perfect repentance unto thy presence. Blessed art thou, O Lord, who delightest in repentance.

VI. Forgive us, O our Father, for we have sinned; pardon us, O our King, for we have transgressed; for thou dost pardon and forgive. Blessed art thou, O Lord, who art gracious, and dost abundantly forgive.

VII. Look upon our affliction and plead our cause, and redeem us speedily for thy name's sake; for thou art a mighty Redeemer. Blessed art thou, O Lord, the Redeemer of Israel.

VIII. Heal us, O Lord, and we shall be healed; save us and we shall be saved; for thou art our praise. Vouchsafe a perfect healing to all our wounds; for thou, almighty King, art a faithful and merciful Physician. Blessed art thou, O Lord, who healest the sick of thy people Israel.

IX. Bless this year unto us, O Lord our God, together with every kind of the produce thereof, for our welfare; give a blessing upon the face of the earth. O satisfy us with thy goodness, and bless our year like other good years. Blessed art thou, O Lord, who blessest the years.

X. Sound the great horn for our freedom; lift up the ensign to gather our exiles, and gather us from the four corners of the earth. Blessed art thou, O Lord, who gatherest the banished ones of thy people Israel.

XI. Restore our judges as at the first, and our counsellors as at the beginning; remove from us grief and suffering; reign thou over us, O Lord, thou alone, in lovingkindness and tender mercy, and justify us in judgment. Blessed art thou, O Lord, the King who lovest righteousness and judgment.

XII. And for slanderers let there be no hope, and let all wickedness perish as in a moment; let all thine enemies be speedily cut off, and the dominion of arrogance do thou uproot and crush, cast down and humble speedily in our days. Blessed art thou, O Lord, who breakest the enemies and humblest the arrogant.

XIII. Towards the righteous and the pious, towards the elders of thy people the house of Israel, towards the remnant of their scribes, towards the proselytes of righteousness, and towards us also may thy tender mercies be stirred, O Lord our God; grant a good reward unto all who faithfully trust in thy name; set our portion with them for ever, so that we may not be put to shame; for we have trusted in thee. Blessed art thou, O Lord, the stay and trust of the righteous.

XIV. And to Jerusalem, thy city, return in mercy, and

dwell therein as thou hast spoken; rebuild it soon in our days as an everlasting building, and speedily set up therein the throne of David. Blessed art thou, O Lord, who rebuildest Jerusalem.

XV. Speedily cause the offspring of David, thy servant, to flourish, and let his horn be exalted by thy salvation, because we wait for thy salvation all the day. Blessed art thou, O Lord, who causest the horn of salvation to flourish.

XVI. Hear our voice, O Lord our God; spare us and have mercy upon us, and accept our prayer in mercy and favour; for thou art a God who hearkenest unto prayers and supplications; from thy presence, O our King, turn us not empty away; for thou hearkenest in mercy to the prayer of thy people Israel. Blessed art thou, O Lord, who hearkenest unto prayer.

XVII. Accept, O Lord our God, thy people Israel and their prayer; restore the service to the oracle of thy house; receive in love and favour both the fire-offerings of Israel and their prayer; and may the service of thy people Israel be ever acceptable unto thee. And let our eyes behold thy return in mercy to Zion. Blessed art thou, O Lord, who restorest thy divine presence unto Zion.

XVIII. We give thanks unto thee, for thou art the Lord our God and the God of our fathers for ever and ever; thou art the Rock of our lives, the Shield of our salvation through every generation. We will give thanks unto thee and declare thy praise for our lives which are committed unto thy hand, and for our souls which are in thy charge, and for thy miracles, which are daily with us, and for thy wonders and thy benefits, which are wrought at all times, evening, morn and noon. O thou who art all-good, whose mercies fail not; thou, merciful Being, whose lovingkindnesses never cease, we have ever hoped in thee. For all these things thy name, O our King, shall be continually blessed and exalted for ever and ever. And everything that liveth shall give thanks unto thee for ever, and shall praise thy name in truth, O God, our salvation and our help. Blessed art thou, O Lord, whose name is All-good, and unto whom it is becoming to give thanks.

XIX. Grant peace, welfare, blessing, grace, lovingkindness and mercy unto us and unto all Israel, thy people. Bless us, O our Father, even all of us together, with the light of thy countenance; for by the light of thy countenance thou hast given us, O Lord our God, the Law of life, lovingkindness and righteousness, blessing, mercy, life and peace; and may it be good in thy sight to bless thy people Israel at all times and in every hour with thy peace. Grant abundant peace unto Israel thy people for ever; for thou art the sovereign Lord of all peace; and may it be good in thy sight to bless thy people Israel at all times and in every hour with thy peace. Blessed art thou, O Lord, who blessest thy people Israel with peace.[7]

The Nature of the Benedictions

If we are to consider the influence of the Eighteen Benedictions upon the prayers and prayer life of Jesus, particularly upon the Lord's Prayer, we should note the

[7] Translations are from *The Authorized Daily Prayer Book*, ed. S. Singer (9th ed.; London: Eyre and Spottiswoode, 1912), pp. 44-54.

subjects involved. The whole gamut of man's religious needs is covered here. Just as in the Lord's prayer, both his spiritual and material necessities are included.

When one prays these prayers he is praying for moral knowledge (IV), repentance and forgiveness (V, VI), deliverance from affliction and for healing (VII, VIII), material blessings and "every kind of produce" (IX), restoration of the Kingdom (X, XIV, XV, XVII), consolation and victory over one's enemies (XI, XII), and for peace (XIX).

Distinctions have been noted between the various sections of the series. The first ones are personal; next come general petitions for the welfare of the nation and its people; the final section deals with thanksgiving.

In the Benedictions God is addressed twice as "Father" (V, VI). This is significant when we note how the Lord's Prayer opens. The beginning of the Jewish prayer for the New Year also calls God "Father." Produce is mentioned (IX) just as "daily bread" is in the Lord's Prayer. Forgiveness is also sought (VI), which is likewise reminiscent of the Lord's Prayer.

More important, however, than these specific parallels between the Eighteen Benedictions and the Lord's Prayer of Jesus is the community of spirit between them. Since Jesus grew up within the environment of the synagogue, probably went to school there and attended its services, he was undoubtedly so familiar with these Benedictions that he must have known them by heart. Their influence upon his own prayer life could not but have been considerable.

44

The Kaddish

Other prayers were used in the synagogue service besides the Eighteen Benedictions. These too would make their impression on a growing lad, just as they would be meaningful to an adult. They also would be a part of Jesus' own religious experience and contribute to his prayer life and to his teachings on prayer.

One of these was the Kaddish. Judged by its use, it too belongs in its significance with the Shema and the Benedictions. Its use in the synagogue has been compared with the use of the Lord's Prayer in Christian worship.[8] At different points in the service it was read aloud by the "reader," and the congregation followed responsively with "Amen." There was a longer and a shorter form.

The Kaddish reads:

Magnified and sanctified be His great name in the world which He hath created according to His will. May He establish His Kingdom during your life and during your days, and during the life of all the House of Israel, even speedily and at a near time, and say ye Amen.

Parallels between the Kaddish and the Lord's Prayer may be clearly seen in the references in the former to God's name being sanctified. As we shall see later in considering the opening address in Jesus' prayer, the "hallowing" of God's name is most prominent. It sets the mental and spiritual stance for what is to follow.

[8] W. O. E. Oesterley and G. H. Box, *The Religion and Worship of the Synagogue* (New York: Scribners, 1907), p. 339.

Another similarity between the two is in the reference to the Kingdom which each contains. Both prayers petition God for the coming of the Kingdom. The Kaddish says: "May He establish His Kingdom during your life." The Lord's Prayer petitions: "Thy kingdom come, Thy will be done, on earth as it is in heaven" (Matt. 6:10).

Here again, as Jesus phrases the Lord's Prayer, its similarities to the Kaddish should not be regarded as literary borrowing, but as an expression of the same train of thought. Prayer for the Kingdom had become a part of the thought and feeling of Jesus through his synagogue associations. In his own prayer he gave it the imprint of his own mind as he related it to the other petitions that surround it. It was his particular use of it in the light of his total teachings that made it unique.

There was also a special mourner's Kaddish in which the prayer was recited in such a way as to show that the piety of the son who remained on earth was similar to that of the deceased. It was not so much a prayer for the dead as a prayer by the living who mourned. The prayer was offered throughout the year immediately following the parent's death and again at each anniversary.

Morning Prayer

The following brief outline of the morning service of the synagogue is based upon the British translation of the Authorized Daily Prayer Book. Variations were possible as individual prayers were sometimes introduced. While it cannot be established definitely that this is the procedure followed during Jesus' time, it is clear that it rests on ancient tradition and may well represent what he knew. The Shema, the Eighteen Benedictions, and the Kaddish are found here as well as selections from the psalms. The page numbers refer to the edition used.

1. Morning Blessings (pp. 4 ff.)
2. Biblical Passages (pp. a ff., 13-14)
3. Psalms of Praise (pp. 17-36)
4. Half-Kaddish introducing the Shema (pp. 37-44)
5. The Eighteen Benedictions (pp. 44-54)
6. Supplications (pp. 54-62), Psalm 6 (pp. 64-65), and Half-Kaddish
7. Psalms 145 and 20 (pp. 71-75)
8. Full Kaddish (pp. 75-78)
9. The Day's Psalm (pp. 80 ff.)

How many times Jesus attended the Morning Prayer at the synagogue would be difficult, if not impossible, to say. That he was a regular attendant at synagogue services, however, is implied in the Gospels. The frequent participation in such a service would fill the worshiper with a sense of God's presence in the life of men and of his providential acts in history. It would make a difference in the way one prayed, and its contribution to the prayer life of Jesus, even to the contents of the Lord's Prayer, would have been noteworthy.

There were other prayers offered at the synagogue in addition to the major ones. Special observances at particular festival seasons of the year called for additional expressions of prayer. Passover, Pentecost, and Tabernacles necessitated appropriate prayers.[9] These were composed by rabbis or other pious individuals. Some gained a reputation for special gifts in praying.[10]

Jesus' own praying would fall into this category. Again we are left to speculation. But, as the following chapter will indicate, since prayer played such a major role in Jesus' ministry and teaching, it is reasonable to conclude that he was also a "praying member" of the synagogue. He no doubt influenced it whenever he attended, just as it left its mark upon him.

[9] Cf. *The Authorized Daily Prayer Book*, pp. 325 ff.
[10] Cf. G. F. Moore, *Judaism*, II, 2, chap. 2.

Chapter III

Jesus and Praying

The Lord's Prayer cannot be understood or appreciated apart from the background of the praying of the Hebrew people, and it can be interpreted only in relation to Jesus' own practice of prayer and his teaching concerning the life of prayer. Not to do so would be like attempting to separate the Jungfrau from the chain of mountains of which it is a part. Just as each act in a person's life is related in some way to the totality of his actions, so each prayer is a part of the stream of praying that nourishes his being.

49

From Prayer to the Lord's Prayer

The Lord's Prayer is the prayer of a praying person to whom communication with God was immediate and continuous. One who was personally unacquainted with praying could not have uttered it. As E. F. Scott put it: "The prayer he taught his disciples is the final outcome of all his thinking on this central act of worship. . . . There have been many expositions of the Lord's Prayer, but we are thrown back in the end on that which Jesus himself has given us in his various sayings. All that they teach us is illustrated in his prayer." [1]

We noted that the prayers of the men in Israel, as the Bible reports them, are related to the issues of life itself. They were not memorized or formalized such as later in Judaism. Neither were they with Jesus, and this is all the more remarkable because in his day prayer practice had already been solidified or conventionalized. We can see this in the Eighteen Benedictions which, according to talmudic tradition, had been composed by men from the Great Synagogue. In some instances these went back to the time of Jesus himself and gave a kind of fixed pattern for praying. But from the record it would seem that Jesus would have had nothing to do with formalized prayers. He disassociated himself from those who thought they were heard for "their much speaking."

This raises the question as to how formal the Lord's

[1] E. F. Scott, *The Lord's Prayer* (New York: Scribners, 1951), p. 8.

Prayer itself really is. And it further causes us to ask to what extent Jesus himself envisioned a liturgical use of the prayer in acts of worship. This question will be considered later.

A brief listing of typical occasions when Jesus himself prayed will show that he did so in moments of decision, frequently, although not always, at times of crisis, for prayer was the constant attitude of his soul. The word here is "Life"; prayer was the very act of living for Jesus.

The Gospels note that Jesus prayed at his baptism (Luke 3:21-22), at the close of the first day of his ministry at Capernaum (Mark 1:35-38), after healing the leper (Luke 5:12-16), prior to selecting the disciples (Luke 6:12-16), when feeding the five thousand (Mark 6:45-46), on the occasion when Peter confessed his faith in him as the Christ at Caesarea Philippi (Mark 8:27-30), when contemplating on the Mount of Transfiguration his coming death (Luke 9:28-29), when giving the Lord's Prayer (Luke 11:1-4), in the garden of Gethsemane (Mark 14:32-42), and when hanging on the cross (Mark 15:34).

When Giving the Lord's Prayer

Jesus was himself praying at the very time when the disciples asked him to teach them to pray (Luke 11:1-4). We are not told what impulse gave rise to this request.

51

Jesus' attitude in prayer was so impressive that it must have drawn from the disciples words like "we want to pray like you." His countenance at such times revealed the light of heaven itself.

There is an additional note here. They asked to be taught to pray "as John taught his disciples." Matthew places the Lord's Prayer at the heart of the Sermon on the Mount (6:9-13). No reference is made in his Gospel at this point to the praying of either Jesus or John. Nor is there any mention of John's practice of prayer in the New Testament accounts of his ministry. Since the disciples phrased their request in this manner, however, it must be assumed that John himself prayed and also taught his followers to pray, as can be expected of the son of a priest.

The content of John's prayers can only be surmised, since we have no record of them. They were probably in line with his convictions concerning the imminence of the coming Kingdom, and the need to repent in preparation for entering it. They would have been intense prayers, for John's entire ministry was heated and climactic. One's praying is always in line with his personal bent and emotional nature.

When Luke wrote his Gospel (c. A.D. 85) the followers of John the Baptist were still active as a fellowship in pursuit of their founder's goals. Could it be that it was their practice to use formal or "learned" prayers? This may even account for the way the request of the disciples to Jesus was phrased.

A Pertinent Inquiry

It is a pertinent inquiry whether or not the Lord's Prayer was Jesus' own prayer. Did he pray it himself or was it intended for the disciples' use only? If the latter, perhaps it should be called the Disciples' Prayer.

Admittedly we have no record of Jesus' actual use of this prayer on any particular occasion. And on the basis of the dogma of the sinlessness of Jesus, we may question whether he would have uttered the petition for forgiveness which lies at the heart of the prayer, for he had no sins that needed to be forgiven.

On the other hand, with this one exception we find Jesus continually praying for the very things that the Lord's Prayer mentions. And even here in his ministry he prays for the forgiveness of others. Could it be that in the petition for forgiveness Jesus was identifying with all sinners, as he did when he let himself be baptized?

In any case the stamp of his own praying is upon the Lord's Prayer. It is only when the prayer is laid alongside Jesus' personal practice of religion that its deeper meanings become apparent. Here is the structure of his prayer life, bared for all to see. Here are the ideas that undergirded his ministry as the Messiah. Here are the hopes which kept him moving against the tides of opposition. Here is the purpose of his life that took him to the cross at the last. We meet Jesus himself more in the Lord's Prayer than at any point in his teaching, particularly when its phrases are interpreted in the light of his total message. As Günther Bornkamm says: "The Lord's Prayer which Jesus teaches his disciples might truly be called the summary of all his sayings about prayer." [2]

Incentives for Praying

Since the practice of prayer is so universal and has been found on all levels of civilization reaching back into the ancient past, a consideration of the incentives to praying may seem almost superfluous. There is a basic drive in man that causes him to reach out to higher powers or a higher Being. No culture has been uncovered that did not reveal some expression of it.

On the level of self-conscious and purposive living, however, where we reflect upon the reasons for man's activities, prayer comes under scrutiny. Why should I pray? How should I pray? What should I expect from praying? Does it make any difference in life, my life and the lives of others?

At this point Jesus' teachings about the incentives for praying become significant. If, however, one is looking for a philosophical rationale for prayer in an academic sense he is bound to be disappointed. Instead, the reasons are ruggedly personal, stemming mostly from the character of God as Jesus knew him.

[2] Günther Bornkamm, *Jesus of Nazareth*, trans. I. and F. McLuskey and J. M. Robinson (New York: Harper, 1960), p. 136.

For instance, he once inquired whether a father would give a stone to his son who has asked for a loaf, or a serpent if he has requested a fish. Obviously not, evil though we are. "How much more will your Father who is in heaven give good things to those who ask him?" (Matt. 7:9-11.) The argument here is based upon God's fatherly nature; it is the logic of personal character that Jesus urges.

Scattered throughout Jesus' teachings are countless other statements which make faith in prayer plausible, if not all but inevitable. God's knowledge of his children is as detailed as if he had numbered the hairs of their heads (Luke 12:7). Why then "heap up empty phrases" in frantic praying? This is what the unbelieving Gentiles do. Actually, "your Father knows what you need before you ask him" (Matt. 6:7-8).

Added to God's fatherly love and detailed knowledge of his children, both of which are significant incentives to praying, there was in Jesus a tremendous sense of the power of God. Here he found a further reason for praying. In another connection he once said: "With men this [the salvation of the rich] is impossible, but with God all things are possible" (Matt. 19:26). There is no need to pray to a weak God; only a God who can effectively respond will inspire praying.

In another chapter we shall see that the closing line of the Lord's Prayer was added later by the church, possibly to round it out for liturgical purposes. Even so, it must have been regarded as appropriate to the rest of the prayer. It includes a reference to God's power, along with his glory and the kingdom.[3]

How to Pray

Incentives to praying such as God's love, knowledge, and power awaken within man the impulse to pray. But how shall he express this drive toward communication with God in prayer? We have already noted that Jesus did not urge the conventional methods of praying followed in his day, although he prayed frequently. Instead, his praying was the spontaneous, unstilted expression of a free spirit.

On the other hand he does deal with the "how" in terms of attitudes that attend his kind of praying. He spoke, for instance, of *asking, seeking,* and *knocking,* and promised a lively response of *receiving, finding,* and *entering* (Matt. 7:7-8). These should not lead to the fatalistic assumption that, because God cares, knows, and is powerful, all man needs to do is to take what comes. Instead, Jesus invited men to "press with vigor on" in their praying, to put themselves into it, to care enough to be absorbed in this act of communication.

Humility in Praying

But Jesus also believed in the attitude of humility in man's praying. Man's sense of urgency must not lead

[3] Cf. footnote to Matt. 6:13 in RSV.

to self-centered demanding. He speaks of praying to the Father "in secret," of going into the room and shutting the door (Matt. 6:6). This need not mean that Jesus was against public prayer, but rather that he turned from the showy type of praying which was sometimes popular in his day.

Too often Jesus had seen the Pharisee who stood and prayed in public, loudly proclaiming his own righteousness and good deeds, while casting scorn on the publican standing far off, whose only petition was: "God be merciful to me a sinner." So humble was this poor suppliant that he would not lift his eyes to heaven. The Pharisee's prayer did not even get off the ground. As Jesus said of him, "he prayed thus *with himself*" (Luke 18:9-14). The publican was humble; the Pharisee was prideful.

Humility in praying as Jesus proclaimed it shows itself most of all in the willingness to accept God's will rather than to push blatantly for one's own. His teaching here is not only found in the petition of the Lord's Prayer: "Thy will be done on earth as it is in heaven," but also in his own prayer as he faced the cross.

The Garden of Gethsemane represents the supreme illustration of true Christian praying. Jesus drew back from "the cup," as he called it. The cross in all its physical and mental pain was horrendous. And Jesus prayed to be delivered from drinking this bitter draught. He did not hesitate to say to the Father exactly what was in his heart on this occasion; he spoke up and did not hold back. There was such openness between himself and God that he was free to bare his soul without being presumptuous. But having done this, he added: "Nevertheless not my will, but thine, be done" (Luke 22:39-46). Humility such as this is a far cry from the kind of praying that seeks to bend God's will to man's desire.

Persistence in Praying

Humility in praying, however, did not mean to Jesus that men should pray in an apathetical fashion. There was such a thing as taking the Kingdom by force and even violence (Matt. 11:12).

For instance, Jesus had almost an obsessive concern (in the best sense) with the need for men to persist in the things of the Kingdom. He insisted that it be placed first in the priorities of life (Matt. 6:33), given the highest value of all life's values (Matt. 13:44-46), and he counseled that men should strive (agonize) to enter it (Luke 13:24). Nothing should interfere, neither eyes nor hands nor feet (Matt. 18:8-9). Even when Jesus was speaking symbolically, his seriousness cannot be missed.

Within such an outlook prayer too became a persistent pursuit. The "twin" prayer parables of the Friend at Midnight (Luke 11:5-8) and the Importunate Widow (Luke 18:1-8) tell of persons who persisted in their requests to others (the first for bread and the second for justice) until they received a response. And receive it they did!

It is easy to conclude that by begging and whining one can secure his desires even from an unwilling heaven.

But this interpretation would deny Jesus' conviction that men should pray within the will of God. The reason for such persistence must lie elsewhere, not in God but in ourselves. Men need to remain eager and earnest in their prayer life for their own sakes.

As God's children persist they mature in understanding. As they wait intently upon God, they may discover that they can answer their own prayer or grow up to handle it when it comes. Again, they may conclude that there is a better way than they had thought. But most of all they will participate in a communion with God that is in itself an answer. The main fact in all this area of prayer is that God is a loving, knowing, and mighty Father, as eager and willing to respond to his children's deepest necessities as is air to rush in and fill a vacuum.

Prayer and the Answer

In all praying the answer looms large. The lower magical levels stress one's getting what he requests in the very terms in which it is sought. Some of the statements in the Gospels, if taken by themselves, seem to promise this. Such a word is: "And whatever you ask in prayer, you will receive, if you have faith" (Matt. 21:22). Another such statement of Jesus is: "If two of you agree on earth about anything they ask, it will be done for them by my Father in heaven" (Matt. 18:19). These are quoted by Christians over and over again, sometimes in the anguish of prayer for deliverance.

Receiving an answer is, however, contingent upon certain conditions. The first is that the prayer must be offered in faith. And the second is that a pact between believers must be made. But what does faith mean in such an instance, and how does a prayer pact become effective?

Faith as Jesus understands it must be interpreted within the total context of Jesus' teaching concerning God, man, and the Kingdom. It is a moral attitude in relation to God as a living righteous Father who seeks what is best for his children. To pray "in faith" is to trust God, to know that he hears our petitions and will respond in love as he wills what is best.[4]

Within such an approach to praying, making a prayer pact with another is not a kind of manipulation of God to force his hand. Instead, it is establishing a fellowship in faith that quickens the spiritual relationships in prayer. Each helps to deepen the faith of the other, to bring an attitude of trustful dependence. It is not what it does to God's intentions but what it makes possible within man's.

The Gospel of John has captured the spiritual understanding of such statements in its prayer promises. Its reassurances that prayer is answered are some of the strongest in the New Testament. And their phrasing

[4] Note George A. Buttrick's statement in this regard: "He [the praying man] must believe that man is free, that God is near, and good, and mighty, and that the world will yield to their co-working." *Prayer* (Nashville: Abingdon Press, 1942), p. 32.

contains moral safeguards against a magical interpretation of the promise.

First of all, in the Gospel of John prayer is made in Jesus' name: "Whatever you ask *in my name,* I will do it, . . . if you ask anything *in my name,* I will do it" (14:13-14). The divine name was synonymous with the divine nature. To pray in Jesus' name, therefore, is to pray in line with his nature and spirit. This removes selfish desires and limited perspectives from our praying.

Again, in John we find this same built-in condition for praying expressed somewhat differently. Jesus says: "If you abide in me, and my words abide in you, ask whatever you will, and it shall be done for you" (15:7). The point here is that if one abides in spiritual union with Jesus, his will and his Lord's will become one. Therefore his prayer will come out of the very spirit that is divine and alive in his being. Such praying contains its own answer; it is as though Jesus were himself praying in the person who prayed while abiding in him.

Jesus' Personal Prayers

Jesus' teachings concerning prayer were those of a praying person, formed in the womb of his personal experience. Not one theoretical accent mars their living witness.

We should not conclude that he prayed only at the times recorded in the Gospels. Prayer was the constant attitude of his mind and heart. It was not a sporadic recourse in life's frantic hours, soon to be forgotten. Rather, it was an expression of his sonship to God.

The Gospels indicate that at times Jesus withdrew from his active ministry for extended periods of praying that we might call prayer retreats. His recorded prayers are usually quite brief. There was no need to add words to words in order to establish contact with God or to move him to act favorably in his behalf.

The tradition that he entered into praying with his whole being is one of the most deeply entrenched in the New Testament. We find it, for instance, in the book of Hebrews where the author writes: "In the days of his flesh, Jesus offered up prayers and supplications, with loud cries and tears, to him who was able to save him from death, and he was heard for his godly fear" (5:7). This is not the portrait of one for whom prayer was only a perfunctory exercise. Instead, it involved body, mind, and spirit—all three. It was he who prayed like this who gave us the Lord's Prayer.

Chapter IV

The New Testament Versions
of the Prayer

It is not unusual in the Gospels to find variants or
different versions of the same teaching or event. Even in
the account of the feeding of the five thousand which
appears in all four Gospels (Mark 6:32-44; Matt. 14:
13-21; Luke 9:10-17; John 6:1-13), there are differences
in some details. The record of the Beatitudes is another
instance of marked variations (Matt. 5:1-12; Luke 6:17,
20-23).

In the case of the Lord's Prayer the differences between the versions are very noticeable even upon a

cursory examination. Many people are not aware of this, however, because their use of the prayer is limited to its inclusion in liturgical readings or in devotional literature where one form is invariably used: the prayer as it appears in Matthew (6:9-13). The companion reading is found only in Luke (11:2-4). No other New Testament writing contains it, although some have thought that Romans 8:15 and Galatians 4:6 show reflections of it where God is addressed as "Abba! Father!"

Why Only Two Accounts?

At first thought it seems unusual that a statement of Jesus that is as important as this one, particularly a prayer that was used in the liturgy of the earliest church, should not be found elsewhere in the New Testament writings besides in Matthew and Luke. We must remember, however, that the New Testament is not a book of liturgy. Although there are reflections of liturgical forms here and there in its pages, its writings are essentially documents of spiritual counsel and interpretation.

The early Christians read the New Testament documents not to discover prayers for use in personal and public worship, but to find guidance in daily Christian living. There are numerous references to prayer and praying in the New Testament, but no prayers as such which are recommended for use, except the Lord's Prayer. This was sufficient. Here was a prayer that was regarded as coming from Jesus himself; more than this, it was considered to be a model that he had given them.

There is yet another possible reason for the lack of references to the Lord's Prayer outside the two Gospels that contain it. It may be that Jesus was not giving the disciples a formula to be repeated verbatum, but a kind of guide for praying. It is as though he were saying: "These are the kind of things about which it is proper to pray." If this were the case, even though the prayer as it appears has an element of rhythmical accent and a poetic form, the need to refer to it frequently would be lessened.

The fact that Mark and John are Gospels, however, presents a specific case. If two Gospels carried the Lord's Prayer, why did not all four? The answer to this question is that all four Gospels did not contain the same accounts in numerous instances. In fact the only miracle story that each of the four has is that of feeding the five thousand. And even when each of them does present the same event, they do not give identical accounts. The individual author often develops his material in his own way; he may have received it through a different channel and in a different form.

There was always the possibility that the Lord's Prayer was so well known that Mark and John, who do not give it, did not feel that it was necessary to do so. Besides, there may be reflections of it in their Gospels, as when Mark reports Jesus' saying that men should watch and pray not to enter into temptation (14:38), and when John notes that Jesus prayed "Father, glorify thy name" (12:28). These contain haunting reminders of phrases and ideas in the Lord's Prayer.

The Two Versions

The two versions of the Lord's Prayer differ not only in the form of the statement, but also in length and situational background. A comparison on all three counts is interesting and revealing.

In Luke, the prayer is found in the special section of the Gospel where the author places tradition or material which he alone for the most part uses. This section is sometimes called the "greater interpolation," and we find it in 9:51–18:14.[1]

Whenever we have accounts of the same event or teaching in Matthew and Luke alone, it is frequently held that it came from a common source, one that Mark did not use. Such an instance is the account of the temptations of Jesus, where Mark carries only a brief reference but the other two give a developed record of three separate issues between Satan and Jesus.[2] The letter Q is assigned to this source, the first letter of the German word *Quelle*, meaning "source." This material is extensive throughout the Gospels, although there is no universal agreement as to its exact content. No copy of such a document, if it were written, as most scholars hold, is in existence today.

Did the Lord's Prayer as found in Matthew and Luke come from Q? It probably did not. The form of the

[1] Cf. "the lesser interpolation," 6:20-8:3.
[2] Cf. Matt. 4:1-11; Mark 1:12-13; Luke 4:1-13. Another instance would be the content of the preaching of John the Baptist in Matt. 3:1-12; Mark 1:3-8; Luke 3:2-17.

two accounts varies more than usual in the use of Q. This variation requires a deeper explanation than that, though borrowed from a common source, they were recorded by two different authors.

A sounder suggestion is that, although each version of the prayer goes back to an actual statement made by Jesus, they were remembered and transmitted differently. Ernst Lohmeyer holds that from the very beginning the Lord's Prayer was handed down in two forms.[3] The meter of the version in Matthew is reminiscent of the prophets and psalmists. It may have a Galilean background. That of Luke's version is more Aramaic in character and may have a broader Palestinian source. Lohmeyer further suggests that the reason Matthew's form became the one officially used in the church was due to the authority, in this instance, of Galilee, although in other regards Jerusalem slowly won a position of prestige.

Further Considerations

Before discussing further the two forms of the Lord's Prayer, it would be well to view them side by side:[4]

[3] Ernst Lohmeyer, *Our Father*, trans. J. Bowden (New York: Harper, 1966), p. 293.

[4] This chart was taken from the article on the "Lord's Prayer" by C. W. F. Smith in *The Interpreter's Dictionary of the Bible*, hereafter referred to as IDB (Nashville: Abingdon Press, 1962), III, 154.

Matt. 6	Luke 11
9a Pray then like this:	2a when you pray, say:
b Our Father	b Father,
c who art in heaven,	
d may thy name be hallowed;	c may thy name be hallowed;
10a May thy kingdom come;	d May thy kingdom come;
b May thy will come to pass	
c as in heaven so also on earth;	
11a Our bread for the morrow	3a Our bread for the morrow
b give us today;	b give us day by day;
12 And forgive us our debts, as we also have forgiven our debtors;	4a And forgive us our sins, for we ourselves also forgive all who are indebted to us;
13a And do not lead us into temptation,	b And do not lead us into temptation.
b but deliver us from evil (or, the evil one)	
c Some MSS of Matthew (W, H, 13, bg etc., Byz., Sy^e, Sa, Did.) contain an added doxology: "because thine is the kingdom and the power and the glory for ever."	

68

The question is sometimes asked as to which was the original form of the Lord's Prayer. If we assume that either Matthew's or Luke's was the original, or nearly so, which shall it be? Matthew and Luke are both usually dated somewhere in the ninth decade of the first century; it is impossible to tell which was written earlier, although reasonable attempts have been made to do so. In addition, it is quite unlikely that the authors involved here were acquainted with each other's work. Had they been, why would the later author have neglected to use the special or individual material carried in the earlier (whichever this was)?

We are left, therefore, to a comparison of the two forms of the prayer itself as we seek to determine which was more likely the original. Usually in such determinations, when we have two versions of the same statement or event, one longer than the other, the shorter form is considered the earlier. The tendency to enlarge an account, either by way of interpretation or simply to tell a more impressive tale, leads to this conclusion.

In regard to the Lord's Prayer many scholars consider the shorter Lucan form as the earlier, perhaps original, form of the prayer. Did not Jesus urge brevity in praying? Would not the poetic form of Matthew's version argue for some formalizing or shaping by the community as it sought to use the prayer liturgically, thus making it a later version? And would not interpretive additional phrases help the new communicant in the church to understand better what Jesus meant in the prayer? An affirmative answer to these questions is difficult to avoid.

However, E. F. Scott argues quite impressively for the priority of Matthew's version.[5] In handling historical tradition, passages may be shortened as well as lengthened. Matthew's version is not too replete with words; there is nothing embroidered or elaborate in its statements. By contrast, Luke is abrupt and does not have the poetic quality that characterizes so many of Jesus' teachings. One should expect, in addition to the Jewish accents found in Matthew's version, others which Luke seems to remove from the prayer. The fact that the Didache, a manual of church order of the middle of the second century A.D., carries Matthew's form rather than Luke's indicates the customary use in that day. It also suggests that Matthew "gives the words of Jesus as nearly as they could be remembered by those who heard them first." [6]

The increasing conviction among scholars is that its liturgical use in worship is somewhat responsible for its form. The doxology "for thine is the kingdom and the power and the glory for ever," appended to Matthew's version, can best be understood as necessary for a liturgical adaptation. The Didache which follows Matthew contains the doxology, but not all of it. The word "kingdom" is omitted, and also the final "Amen." These came even later, it would seem, suggesting a development in liturgical use. The Didache also adds: "Pray thus three times a day."

[5] *The Lord's Prayer*, pp. 27 ff.
[6] *Ibid.*, p. 30.

A Community Prayer

The Lord's Prayer is a prayer for the Christian community. Both versions clearly indicate this. The "Our" with which it begins in Matthew and continues in both Matthew and Luke is inclusive. The same may be seen in the use of the word "us" in connection with forgiveness and temptation.

This is not to say that the Christian community rather than Jesus composed the prayer. It is a reflection of Jesus' feeling for his followers as the people of God who should continue to pray together as they had done for many centuries. His own experience as a part of the worshiping community at the synagogue or the Temple made this for him a natural approach to praying. Jesus had been reared to pray with his brothers in Israel. He believed that they should continue thus to pray in the New Israel of the Kingdom he was even now inaugurating.

The settings for giving the Lord's Prayer, though different in Matthew and Luke, further underscore its character as a community prayer. Luke says that the disciples asked Jesus to teach them to pray (11:1). This was more than a general request for encouraging words about prayer, such as we find in his parables and sayings. It was more like: "Give us a prayer." Matthew placed the Lord's Prayer at the heart of the Sermon on the Mount. Jesus had been condemning the prayer practices of those who "heap up empty phrases" in their praying. In contrast to this method he said: "Pray then like this:" and

71

followed with the Lord's Prayer. In both cases the setting suggests that Jesus was giving group instruction for group praying.

Which was the true setting? Did Jesus give the prayer twice? The answer to these questions is not clear. When we consider, however, that Matthew presents in the Sermon on the Mount some sayings of Jesus that are found in a different and preferred setting in the other Gospels, the presumption is strong that he might be doing the same here. In this case, Luke's setting would be the more likely instead of the didactic framework of the sermon. It is more personal and intimate, contains a reference to the practice of John the Baptist, and fits into the custom of the Jews in Jesus' time who used formal prayer three times daily.

Did Jesus give the prayer twice? One cannot categorically rule out this possibility. The situation is somewhat similar in regard to the Cleansing of the Temple. The Synoptic Gospels place this event at the beginning of the last week of Jesus' life (Matt. 21:12-13; Mark 11:15-17; Luke 19:45-46). John's Gospel has it at the beginning of his public ministry (John 2:13-17). In this case scholars are divided in their conclusion, some holding to the Synoptic view, others to the Johannine, and still others favor the conclusion that Jesus cleansed the Temple on two separate occasions.

The Lord's Prayer, however, is usually considered in terms of a single giving of the prayer reported in two different versions. Luke's more personal setting is mostly the preferred one. Yet Matthew's issue of lengthy prayers and showy praying versus a succinct, direct, and brief prayer makes his version not at all unrealistic. It is typical of Jesus' teaching on prayer elsewhere and of his general attitude toward religious practices.

How Many Petitions?

In comparing Matthew's and Luke's versions of the Lord's Prayer, the number of separate petitions involved must be discussed. Here again different conclusions are possible: In Matthew's version, for instance, where do the petitions begin? Is the opening address a petition? Is only the last part of the verse, i.e. "Hallowed be thy name," a petition? Perhaps the entire verse is just an ascription of praise to God as one begins to pray. Its purpose would then be to create in the mind of the one praying a proper attitude.

If we assume that the opening statement is not a separate petition, we will have requests for the coming of the Kingdom, for bread, forgiveness, and strength for overcoming temptation, making a total of four. But what of the words: "Thy will be done, on earth as it is in heaven," and: "But deliver us from evil"? Are they individual petitions, or explications of the petitions for the Kingdom and for help in times of temptation? As such they would be regarded as examples of Hebraic poetic parallelism. This is my assumption, and I also regard "Hallowed be thy name" as a part of the address and not as a separate petition. If each of these, however, were considered as a separate petition, the number would be seven.[7]

Whatever one decides concerning the number of petitions in the prayer, the fact remains that they are few. In examining them in detail we shall discover that they are basic to life and provide a check against the multiple impulses that rise within us to ask for this or that or the other thing that the passing moment seems to make desirable.

Some Difference in Wording

Thus far we have been considering the broad differences between the versions of the Lord's Prayer in Matthew and Luke. We have dealt with such matters as the setting of the prayer, its length, the original form in which it was given, its liturgical aspects, community, character, and the number of petitions. There are in addition some specific variations in wording where the same petition is found that should also be indicated at this point, even though they will be touched upon later. Here again the question as to what Jesus really said comes to the fore. And here again we are left with several alternatives. Such matters enrich the prayer as they reveal unplumbed depths of possibilities in its meaning.

In the petition for bread, Matthew's version tells us to pray: "Give us this day our daily bread," with the alternate reading in the footnote of "our bread for the morrow."

[7] The IDB considers the number to be six, while E. F. Scott speaks of "The Seven Petitions."

In this way the petitioner is asking for a giving that goes on and on unceasingly. There was a tomorrow to be considered.

Luke phrases it differently: "Give us each day our daily bread." This is reminiscent of God's sending the manna in the wilderness where the gift was for the present day (Exod. 16:13 ff.). The people were told to eat the daily supply when given because the manna would spoil (vs. 20) if they attempted to carry it over for another day. More would be given when the morrow came, but today's bread was for today. Therefore, "Morning by morning they gathered it" (vs. 21).

There is a further variation between Matthew's and Luke's versions in the petition for forgiveness. In 6:12a, Matthew has the word "debts" (opheilemata), where Luke in 11:4a has "sins" (hamartias). The familiar word "trespasses" (paraptomata), used in some liturgical forms, is not found in the prayer itself but appears in Matthew 6:14-15. Luke's additional statement (vs. 4b) uses the word "indebtedness" as Matthew uses "debts," so the difference between the two versions here is probably more apparent than real. The Jews customarily regarded sins as debts in any case. Matthew's reading may, therefore, be more true to the original than Luke's. In the Didache, the words "our debt" replace "our debts." The singular here may suggest man's constant sinful character rather than the sins daily committed.

A third specific variation is found in the petition for forgiveness. Matthew adds: "As we also have forgiven" (vs. 12b), while Luke has: "for we ourselves forgive" (vs. 4b). In the English translation, Matthew seems to refer to past acts of forgiveness and Luke to a present act or daily attitude of willingness to forgive.[8] It does not rule out, however, an intention to forgive in the future.

The variations between Matthew's and Luke's versions, both general and detailed, do not suggest that there were two separate prayers. Rather they are best accounted for in terms of their background of transmission, liturgical use, teaching function, and community understanding. They are the Lord's Prayer in both Gospels, even as they are today.

[8] Some have suggested that Matthew's use of the aorist tense in Greek may imply that there will be a limit to man's forgiveness of others, depending upon their attitude or actions.

Chapter V

The Address

There is an interesting similarity between the Ten Commandments and the Lord's Prayer. Each in its own way was an instrument for guiding, clarifying, and giving meaning to the religion of those who followed the faiths they represented. The Jews based the law of Israel upon the commandments; the Christians found their spiritual focus through using the prayer that Jesus taught them.

Another similarity is that both the commandments and the prayer open with considerations regulating the relation of man to God and then move on to matters that concern daily living in relation to one's fellowmen. This recognizes that the character of the God who is worshiped determines the very nature of the religion that is practiced. If God is limited in his concern, irresponsible in his decisions, and incoherent in his judgments, those who follow him will be likewise. The most essential element in any religion is the character of the God to whom its adherents look.

It is also true that unless, as in the commandments and in the prayer, one's religion exhibits a responsibility to others, it will become narrowly selfish, ingrown, and fruitless. When, therefore, the decalogue takes a stand against lying, stealing, killing, and covetousness, and the Lord's Prayer insists that forgiving others is basic to experiencing forgiveness oneself, it makes possible a religion of inclusive love and light.[1]

"Our Father"

Sometimes it is held that the uniqueness of the Christian religion lies in its concept of God as Father. This has been a source of inspiration to countless multitudes through the centuries and has been so predominantly true of the Christian's outlook, as over against the ad-

[1] The fact that the Ten Commandments were originally conceived as relating only to the people of God in a narrow sense does not invalidate this principle. In time it was seen to be a universal responsibility.

herents of other religions, that we have assumed that somehow it was our unique heritage.

In a very special sense this is true. No religion in history has made the conception of God as Father as determinative as has Christianity. It has been basic to our teaching concerning providence, forgiveness, social responsibility, prayer, and eternal life. It has been asserted in the face of widely proposed impersonal conceptions of God such as H. N. Wieman's substitute of "interaction," Alfred North Whitehead's principle of "concretion," or the quasi-impersonal "ground of being" of Paul Tillich.

One of the reasons that the practical judgment of Christians rejects these impersonal views of God is that they do not provide an adequate basis for praying, and the personal quality of their experiences in prayer seems to belie them. Any theological idea that does not enrich the prayer experience of Christians is certain to be suspect. It may achieve a current vogue of sorts, but in the long last it will not prevail. The concept of God as Father has persisted in large measure because it has spoken to the religious needs of men as they prayed.

God as Father in Ancient Greek Culture

In spite of all this, Christianity was not the first of the religions and philosophies to think of God as Father. Homer, in about the ninth century B.C., refers to "Father Zeus who rules over the gods and mortal men." He even addresses Zeus as the "father of gods and of men." And about five centuries later Cleanthes the Stoic wrote a hymn to Zeus in which he referred to Zeus as father and urged him to help his children in their misery, saying: "Scatter, O Father, the darkness from their souls." The prayer continues to beseech Zeus to grant them "true understanding." [2]

We should not conclude, however, that the use of the word "father" in these instances implies all that Jesus meant in the opening address of The Lord's Prayer. Words must be read in the light of the background of the times in which they are uttered, as well as over against the character and outlook of the person speaking them. And fatherhood in the ancient Greek civilizations was not fatherhood in the Christian sense as Jesus understood it. The Greek idea of father when applied to a god was mostly that of a ruler, a creator of the universe and the overseer of the household of deities. It lacked, for the most part, the warmth of a personal relation to individuals which Jesus had in mind when he said: "Our Father."

God as Father in the Old Testament

The Old Testament also referred to God as Father. Here again there are particular meanings attached to the term. God is the creator of his special people Israel. He "elected" her to be his own. She was his "first-born son" (cf. Exod. 4:22-23). Israel could say of God: "Thou,

[2] Cf. F. C. Grant, ed., *Hellenistic Religions; the Age of Syncretism* (Indianapolis: Bobbs-Merrill Co. [Liberal Arts Press], 1953), pp. 152 ff.

O Lord, art our Father, our Redeemer, from of old is thy name" (Isa. 63:16c).

Not only is God thought of here as the father of the nation, but he is also regarded as the father of the king. Thus in psalm 2:7 we read: "He said to me, 'You are my son, today I have begotten you.'" As the king's father, God will make the nations the king's heritage and the ends of the earth his possession, and the king shall break Israel's enemies with a rod of iron (vss. 8-9).

It is no wonder that in the New Testament messianic ideas were associated with God's fatherhood as announced in the Old Testament. In his sermon at Antioch in Pisidia Paul applies the second psalm to Jesus as the promised messiah (Acts 13:33). The author of Hebrews finds in the same words the appointment of Christ as high priest. Here ideas of sonship, messiahship, and high priest comingle, each under God as "Father."

It would not be correct to say that God's fatherhood in the Old Testament is invariably present in terms of his relation to the nation alone. Psalm 103:13-14 says: "As a father pities his children, so the Lord pities those who fear him. For he knows our frame; he remembers that we are dust." Such a statement has a singular accent, so that a person as an individual may find strength and hope in it. Yet this particular psalm opens with a reference to God's revelation to Moses and, before it closes, specifically mentions God's steadfast love for those "who keep his covenant and remember to do his commandments" (vs. 18).

God as Father in Jesus' Teaching

Although the thought of God as Father did not begin with Jesus and is not limited to the Judaic-Christian tradition, it took on a new meaning in our Lord's hands. Here is a warmth and personal accent that is lacking in the references we have previously noted. Such warmth Jesus intended when he taught men to pray "Our Father."

Ideas are nurtured in the womb of personal experience, be it in the case of Jesus or of others. It was not because Jesus found God referred to as Father in the Old Testament that he took over the term. Rather he called God "Father" because he realized that he was his father in his own life and ministry.

It was as the Son (the Messiah) that Jesus knew God to be "Father." The New Testament tradition is rich at this point, particularly in the account given by Matthew. Edward Blair has pointed out that the term "Father" in reference to God occurs some forty-five times in Matthew, seventeen of these in the form of "my Father." With some of these the word "heavenly" or "who is in heaven" is found. Eighteen times the words "your Father" occur, while "our Father" appears only in the Lord's Prayer. In addition there are two references to "Father" alone, five to "the Father" and one each to "his Father" and "their Father." Mark carries the word "Father" for God only four times and Luke only fifteen.[3]

---

[3] Cf. Edward P. Blair, *Jesus in the Gospel of Matthew* (Nashville: Abingdon Press, 1960), p. 58.

The Gospel of John shows a particular sensitivity to Jesus' use of the term Father. There are around one hundred and seven examples of such a usage. Some scholars have felt that perhaps this represents the author's particular fondness for the term, rather than Jesus' actual usage. Among these is T. W. Manson who in his work on the teachings of Jesus suggests that the primitive records did not reflect it. He pointed out that Matthew introduces the word Father at least six times into sayings from Q.[4] The supposition is that he may also have done so in other strata of the tradition.

Whether the multiple references to God as Father in their various forms in Matthew and John are historical in the specific instances where they are used, or whether they are due to the authors' interest in the term—there must have been a firm general tradition that it was Jesus' favorite word for God. The Gospel writers felt free to introduce it wherever it seemed appropriate because they were convinced of Jesus' strong feeling for it. His personal thought and religious conviction underlie the word.

It would be difficult to say just when Jesus' realization that God was his Father began to motivate his life. It is like the growing consciousness of self-identity in every person. With some it develops earlier than with others. There is, of course, the tradition, that Luke alone carries, of the visit of Jesus to the Temple at the age of twelve. There he replies to the worried questions of his parents who thought he had been lost: "How is it that you

[4] Cf. T. W. Manson, *The Teaching of Jesus* (New York: Cambridge University Press, 1935), p. 100.

sought me? Did you not know that I must be in my Father's house?" (Luke 2:49.)[5] No doubt some statement of Jesus at this time having to do with God as Father was remembered. And as it was reported, it is quite likely the church regarded it as a messianic assertion.

At his baptism Jesus heard God say that he was his "beloved Son." This is a reflection of psalm 2:7 which as we have already noted originally implied that God was a father—a special father to the king who was ruling or about to rule. The church regarded it as messianic, although the Hebrews had not so considered it.[6] They interpreted Jesus' religious experience at his baptism as an instance of messianic realization.

From this time on the Gospel records present Jesus as thinking of God as Father. This is reflected in the Lord's Prayer as well as in the high-priestly prayer of John 17 where in a mystical fashion Jesus' thought comingles with that of the author as he writes. There is an interesting progression of realization of the character of God as Father in this prayer. First he prays, "*Father*, glorify thou me . . ." (vs. 5). As his sense of God's presence envelops him further he prays, "*Holy Father*, keep them [the disciples] in thy name" (vs. 11). Finally in what

[5] The familiar translation "about my Father's business" is not erroneous. "House" fits better, however, since the question has to do with location. In any case, it is God as his *Father* that makes the issue.

[6] Cf. William Manson, *Jesus the Messiah* (Philadelphia: The Westminster Press, 1946), pp. 149-50.

seems to be almost an outburst of confidence he says, "O *righteous Father,* the world has not known thee, but I have known thee; and these know that thou hast sent me" (vs. 25). From "Father," through "Holy Father," to "O righteous Father" is a journey in experiencing God that was true of Jesus in his ministry whoever reported it, John or the Synoptics.

Father of Whom?

The uniqueness of the relationship between Jesus as "Son" to God as "Father" should not obscure his many references to the universal fatherhood of God. He is the father of all men. As Bultmann forcibly says: "He [God] is the power, here and now, who as Lord and Father *enfolds every man*—limiting and commanding him" (italics mine).[7] In this respect Jesus moves beyond traditional Judaism with an inclusiveness that was unique in his day.

We have noted that eighteen times the expression "your Father" occurs in Jesus' words. Sometimes these are in connection with teachings concerning prayer. This is doubly significant because the true test of the validity of an idea in Christianity is whether or not it can become a working concept in prayer. If not, it does not ring true.

Jesus speaks of receiving a reward from *"your* Father who is in heaven" (Matt. 6:1); he refers to *"your* Father who sees in secret" (6:4); he commands men to "pray to

[7] Rudolf Bultmann: *Theology of the New Testament,* trans. K. Grobel (New York: Scribners, 1951-54), I, 23.

your Father" (6:6); he notes that "*your* heavenly Father feeds" [the birds] (6:26); and he tells men to be perfect "as *your* heavenly Father is perfect" (5:48). This cluster of statements from the Sermon on the Mount helps us to understand why Jesus opened the Lord's Prayer with the words: "Our Father who art in heaven."

Other general teachings could be pointed out which further provide a background for this address. The parable of the Prodigal Son (Luke 15) makes its point by comparing God with the human father who forgives. The assurance that God will answer prayer as surely as an earthly father will respond to a son's request for a loaf or a fish is based on a similar comparison (Luke 11:11-13). Father! Father! Father! from beginning to end permeates the gospel; it is both its strength and its fragrance. In prayer, therefore, the word "Father" leaps to the lips of the Christian as naturally as it does to a child in his own home.

When Will God's Fatherhood Be Revealed?

Most of us speak of God and to God as "Father" in the midst of life's ongoing round of experiences. Yesterday he was our Father; today he is our Father; tomorrow he will be our Father. With the expectancy of a continuing stream of life we use the daily language of children. This is the way in which we pray the Lord's Prayer, as we begin with its opening address. Crises come and go but life continues. Thus it is with God's fatherhood.

There are those, however, who take a particularized view of Jesus' meaning in the Lord's Prayer. They see it as a prayer belonging to the end of the age, an eschatological prayer. Time is reaching its fulfillment; God will move as judge and deliverer, bringing the present order of life to a close. It is somewhat difficult, however, to think of God as an eschatological Father. The idea of a judge, an avenger of evil, or a warrior like the warrior-Messiah at the battle of Armageddon (Rev. 19:11-16) seems not to fit the prayer.

Ernst Lohmeyer, however, interprets the Lord's Prayer in its entirety within an apocalyptic setting, including even the address "Father." He writes: "Here too, we touch on a deeper thought, which brings us nearer to the eschatological idea of this Fatherhood. For what it describes is the onset of the eschatological age, when the poor and the persecuted will be blessed and those who have hitherto been excluded from it will receive salvation. This certainly is, then, simply a consequence of the eschatological Fatherhood of God." [8]

Such interpretations move within the framework of a view of Jesus as a thoroughgoing apocalyptist, and with the assumption that all that Jesus said must be read within this outlook. Therefore every petition within the Lord's Prayer too will be seen to be apocalyptic and eschatological. The logic followed is understandable when one accepts the premise on which it is based. It

[8] Ernst Lohmeyer, *Our Father*, p. 46.

does, however, appear to force words into meanings which in themselves they do not require.

God does not wait to be a special kind of Father till the end of the age when he moves to set up a new order of life. He has been fatherly all along, fully Father at all times. New situations may arise within which he will express his character as a father in unique and even startling ways, but the prayer "Our Father" may be offered for the present with no loss of meaning and relevancy.

Whom Does "Our" Include?

The word "our" in the address of the Lord's Prayer as found in Matthew is significant (6:9). Luke has the single word "Father." This is probably nearer to the "Abba" of the Aramaic which Jesus customarily used (cf. Mark 14:36). It too is sometimes translated "our father," therefore it would seem that the difference between Matthew's version and Luke's here is not so great as it appears to be. Whom does "our" include? This is the important question.

Is Jesus including himself with the disciples in this address? The answer is probably "no" and "yes." Since he is, as the New Testament views him, unique in his sonship the "our" would not include his own person. And as a community prayer that he gave his disciples, he himself is apart from the prayer since he is the Lord of the community. On the other hand, he was one with his brothers in the flesh, "being born in the likeness of men"

(Phil. 2:7). In this sense he prayed as they prayed; their Father was his, as his Father was theirs. Even as he was baptized with them he would also pray with them.

Yet another question persists: How broad is the "our" in relation to men? Does it refer only to the twelve to whom the prayer was given? Does it include all the members of the present Christian community? Does it refer only to those who would be blessed in the new age-to-come? Does it move beyond this to take in all created humanity?

The answer to these questions depends upon Jesus' total outlook. If God is the Father of all men, then potentially this is the prayer of all humanity. As such it goes beyond the limitations and particularism of a traditional Jewish prayer. Its inclusiveness is its grandeur as it sets forth the extent of God's love and the goal of salvation in Christ. To say that it is limited to a certain group such as the disciples, or to those who were to experience the new age, or to the members of the present Christian community—to limit it thus would be to change the character of Jesus' message.

"In Heaven"

The phrase "in heaven" must also be interpreted. The background here is Hebraic. It was customary to locate God in the heavens, or above and beyond the firmament (cf. Gen. 1:14). This is reflected in the book of Revelation where the seer goes through an "open door" into heaven (4:1). There he sees God on a throne surrounded

89

by a rainbow and seated before a sea of glass. He rules the universe; before him are heavenly creatures who constitute a kind of court and pay him honor perpetually.

When the worshiper prays to the Father "in heaven," he is filled with confidence and assurance. There is One who is in control of life, who reigns supreme, and who listens to men's prayers. The powers of evil that threaten life will give way before such a God. He is not only exalted in authority, rule, and power; he is also the Father, *our* Father. The sweep of his fatherhood is as broad as his majesty and power.

God's Name to Be Hallowed

The thought world of the Hebrews emphasized the relationship between name and character or nature of being. The author of John's Gospel has Jesus say in his high-priestly prayer: "I have manifested thy [God's] name" (17:6). This means that he has revealed God's very being to them. Now they know what God is like, who God is, and what he will do.

Jesus goes on and prays: "Holy Father, keep them in thy name" (vs. 11). He is again referring to God's nature as Holy Father. As God will continue to exist in this nature, he will continue to relate himself to his children in terms of love and righteousness. They will be "kept" (protected, led, forgiven, saved) in this love.

God's name is to be hallowed; his nature is to be praised, and he is to be held in reverence. "Hallowed be thy name" (Matt. 6:9; Luke 11:2) may be considered as

90

a separate petition or as a part of the address with which the Lord's Prayer opens. In the latter case it prepares the heart and attitude of him who prays to offer the petitions which follow.

The Hebrews had long been concerned with the "proper" approach to God. The rites of purification which they prescribed on certain occasions were intended to prepare them for drawing near to God. In the account of the giving of the Ten Commandments, for instance, Moses "went down from the mountain to the people, and consecrated the people; and they washed their garments" (Exod. 19:14).[9]

Jesus was not a ceremonialist; he did not think it necessary to perform certain rites before approaching God in prayer if the prayer were to be heard. In his personal life he prayed out of the necessity of the moment; his prayers were personal rather than ceremonial. Even so, to him the hallowing of God's name, if prayer were to be real praying, is basic. Not that it might change God's attitude, and certainly not his will as in magic, but it makes the one who prays more susceptible, open, and able to receive God's gifts.

To hallow God's name is in a special sense to be conscious of his holiness. The quality of holiness is difficult to describe. It involves being set apart and can be used of objects as well as of persons. In reference to God it signalizes his righteousness, absolute goodness, and purity. This is what Isaiah felt concerning God when in

[9] Cf. also the purification rituals referred to in Lev. 11–15.

the Temple he "saw the Lord sitting upon a throne, high and lifted up" (Isa. 6:1). The seraphim cried out one to another "Holy, holy, holy is the Lord of hosts" (vs. 3).

To hallow God's name, the Jews were sometimes moved to substitute the word "heaven" for God. Even his name was too holy to pronounce. Some have felt that this is the reason Matthew often uses the expression "kingdom of heaven" instead of "kingdom of God." It is doubtful whether Jesus would have gone this far. His approach to God was warmly personal and respectful, but not stilted or rigid.

Chapter VI

Thy Kingdom Come

It comes as no surprise that immediately following the opening words or address in the Lord's Prayer Jesus should turn to the theme of the kingdom of God. This was the constant concern of his preaching and the motivation of his ministry. He began to fulfill his mission with the words: "The time is fulfilled, and the kingdom of God is at hand; repent, and believe in the gospel" (Mark 1:15).

Since prayer with Jesus was never a theoretical or purely ritualistic matter, it is natural that for him the Kingdom would become a subject for praying. Events were taking place or were to take place in which God would act; his reign among men was becoming a reality. The time was "fulfilled." Not to pray about the Kingdom under these circumstances would be unthinkable; it was the most important subject of all. It is almost as though Jesus rushed into this petition; he could not postpone lifting it up before God.

The Kingdom and the Name

The relationship between the name of God and the kingdom of God is indissoluble. God's "name" is his nature; there is an existential connection here, so that when he expresses himself on earth his very name is involved. It is his name, hallowed and holy, which makes the expected kingdom *his* Kingdom.

A long line of thinking is behind the kingdom hope of the Hebrews. At times it was considered to be a messianic age with the Messiah as the ruling monarch over it (Isa. 9:6-7; 11:1-10). Peace, justice, and good will would prevail. This was God's doing through the Messiah whom he would raise up from among the people. The character (name) of God would be revealed in the nature of the Kingdom.

Again, the Hebrews thought of the Kingdom in terms of a suffering remnant, purified through the pain of affliction. This suffering would lift others who were depressed and in need of redemption. It was during a period of exile and deprivation that this conception of the Kingdom and of the Suffering Servant developed (Isa. 52:13–53:12). It seems that God used the deep anguish of these years to reveal the ideal of redemption through suffering love. His "name" was even then being made known.

Later, it was the conception of the ruling saints of Israel as constituting the Kingdom that was predominant (Dan. 7:13-14). Coming down from the heavens as the apocalyptic Son of man, God's rule would through them be established on earth. This figure of the Son of man was later thought of as an individual heavenly personage (I Enoch 46:3-4; 48:3; 62:5-14).

Not all the people of Israel shared these hopes of the Kingdom as deeply as the prophets who revealed them. Nor did the mass of the people possess an understanding of what they meant in their various forms. But there was in Israel a growing sense of national hope. God's nature would be revealed and their fortunes which had come upon evil days reversed.

There was a core of Hebrew nationalism here. Other nations were for the most part excluded, in spite of Second Isaiah's vision of Israel as a light to the Gentiles (Isa. 49:6). The Kingdom for the Jews was a Jewish hope. They too prayed for its coming. In the Kaddish they offered the petition: "May he establish his kingdom during your life and during your days and during the life of all the house of Israel."

When Jesus Prayed for the Kingdom

When Jesus placed the petition for the coming of the Kingdom in the Lord's Prayer he was not, however, looking to the past but to the present and the future. Its advent was imminent in the things that were already happening. The very air was electric with God's rule.

John the Baptist had said that the ax was laid to the root of the tree *even now*. Jesus' very deeds, as demons were cast out, proclaimed its coming: "If it is by the Spirit of God that I cast out demons, then the kingdom of God has come upon you" (Matt. 12:28). The emissaries from John who had come to inquire whether he were the one who was to come, whose responsibility it was to bring in the Kingdom, were told: "From the days of John the Baptist until now the kingdom of heaven has suffered violence, and men of violence take it by force" (Matt. 11:12). The Kingdom was already here and men were entering it forcefully.

His view of the Kingdom, however, was in many respects unlike the traditional expectations of the Hebrews, and it was likely that some would be offended. Many actually were, and Jesus recognized this fact. There was considerable pathos in his words: "Blessed is he who takes no offense at me" (Matt. 11:6).

As men prayed for the Kingdom's coming on Jesus' terms they were not asking for a restored political order, a Davidic reign with the Jews in the role of God's favored sons among men. Instead they were praying for God's universal rule, for his will to be done on earth as it was done in heaven.

The nonpolitical character of the Kingdom was an unwelcome message to many. The Zealots of Jesus' day, for instance, would look with disfavor upon it, since this group proposed military action as a means for establishing the Kingdom.[1] Not only was it not to be political, but Jesus asked men to pray as a means for its coming. This prayer was not that God would give the victory to Israel's military attempt, but that he would move to establish it through spiritual channels, such as were actually open in the person and ministry of Jesus. The Zealots disagreed with this.

Only the Resurrection with its release of spiritual power was able to convince even the early Christian community that it was not to expect a political rule when the Kingdom came. The "apostles" actually asked the resurrected Christ: "Lord, will you at this time restore the kingdom to Israel?" meaning an earthly political rule (Acts 1:6). Only later did Paul write: "For the kingdom of God . . . [means] righteousness and peace and joy in the Holy Spirit" (Rom. 14:17).

The form of this petition for the coming of the Kingdom in Marcion's New Testament reads: "May thy holy spirit come upon us and cleanse us." This appeared in the middle of the second century when Marcion was in general considered a heretic. Did he deliberately change the wording of "thy kingdom come" because of his views, or was this a form of the petition, as E. F. Scott holds, that was already acceptable among the early church fathers?[2] It seems likely that there was a continual spiritualizing of the petition for the coming of

[1] Cf. W. G. Kümmel, *Promise and Fulfilment*, trans. D. M. Barton (Naperville: Allenson, 1957), pp. 112 ff.

[2] *The Lord's Prayer*, p. 26.

the Kingdom which universalized it and removed any trace of Jewish nationalism which some had been inclined to read into it.

God's Will on Earth

The kingdom of God for which Jesus tells men to pray is the reign of God on earth. Satan's sway is to end; God's will shall be done.[3]

Matthew alone carries the words: "Thy will be done, on earth as it is in heaven" (6:10). "Heaven" here is the site of God's throne (Matt. 5:34-35). The "earth" is his footstool. Heaven, therefore, is nearer to God, even though God has created both. Earth is the place where opposition to God is rampant. It will be brought into line with heaven where moth and rust do not corrupt. Both will ultimately be destroyed (Matt. 5:18) and only God's order will remain. The details are sometimes confusing and overlaid with apocalyptic imagery, but the reference here to God's will supplanting the will of evil men and forces is clear.

The Kingdom reveals the ultimate meaning of history. It is the scene where God's will is being brought to pass. When men obey this will which God has revealed in the commandments and through the prophets (Heb. 1:1)— and now in Jesus the Son—the Kingdom will come. Just how it will come, the prayer itself does not say.

This added petition in Matthew's version of the Lord's

[3] Cf. Rudolf Bultmann, *Theology of the New Testament*, I, 4 ff.

Prayer is in reality an explication of "Thy kingdom come," for it defines the nature of the Kingdom. While it may have been appended to a simpler form of the petition (cf. Luke 11:2) as a poetic parallel to make it liturgically smooth, it serves to deepen an understanding of the character of the Kingdom. It is the will of God on earth as in heaven.[4]

But what is the will of God to which the prayer refers? The prayer does not indicate what is meant except as far as its petitions for daily bread, forgiveness, and deliverance from temptation would imply. Only in the broadest sense, therefore, within the total outlook of Jesus can one say what is meant by the will of God here. The ethos of the Sermon on the Mount, as it has come to be known (Matt. 5–7), would surely be representative of God's will. The Beatitudes with their ideals for Christian living (5:3-11), the summons to keep from murderous thoughts (5:21-26), to hold the marriage vow sacred (5:27-32), to be truthful (5:33-37), to love one's enemies (5:43-48), to pray simply with no display of piety (6:5-8), etc., all these and other commands throughout the Gospels are within the will of God.[5]

There are multiple circumstances in life where decisions must be made. Here too God has a will to be followed. Jesus came upon such a moment when he

[4] Cf. C. F. Burney, *The Poetry of Our Lord* (Oxford: Clarendon Press, 1925), Ch. 2.

[5] For additional references to what comes within the will of God, cf. Matt. 12:50; 18:4; Mark 3:35; John 4:34; 5:30; 6:38-40.

faced the cross and prayed to be delivered from it, adding: "Nevertheless, not as I will, but as thou wilt" (Matt. 26:39). The apostle Paul likewise made numerous decisions in his travels in which he sought and followed the will of God. He would not "speak the word in Asia" at the beginning of his second missionary journey, being forbidden by the Holy Spirit to do so, nor go into Bithynia because "the Spirit of Jesus did not allow them" (Acts 16:6-7). The will of God was the determinative factor in these decisions.[6]

To pray "Thy will be done, on earth as it is in heaven" is to assert a specific view of life. The petition provides a basis from which to move out and face the world. There is a way to live; it is God's way. In praying for it to be realized, one is personally committing his life to that will, freely and without compunction. This is what makes the petition significant.

As he prays for God's will man is expected enthusiastically to pursue it. The church father Chrysostom, in the fourth century A.D., emphasized this in his paraphrase of the petition: "He [Christ] bade us indeed long for the heavenly city, but meanwhile we are to pray *not to do God's will by halves,* but to perform all things as he wills" (italics mine).

We know of a saying by Judah ben Tema in Pirke Aboth: "Be strong as a leopard, and swift as an eagle, and fleet as a hart, and courageous as a lion, to do the will

---

[6] Paul says that it was by the will of God that he became an apostle in the first place (I Cor. 1:1; II Cor. 1:1; Col. 1:1).

of thy Father which is in heaven." Similar words are attributed to Gamaliel: "Do his will as thy will, that he may do thy will as his will. Annihilate thy will before his will, that he may annihilate the will of others before thy will."[7] Obviously these are Hebrew parallels to Jesus' petition.

How Will the Kingdom Come?

How will the Kingdom come? The words of the petition "Thy kingdom come" do not indicate the method of its coming. It says that something lies ahead that is not yet present; it is *to come*. And men are to pray for its coming. This probably also implies that they are to work for its coming (cf. Matt. 7:24-27).

Since these are words of Jesus, they should be interpreted within the context of his total teaching on the Kingdom. His own view and not that of another should determine the meaning of the petition. But at this very point a difficulty arises. Interpreters of Jesus do not agree as to what he said or meant, particularly where his message on the Kingdom is concerned.

Some regard him as predominantly an apocalyptist who thought that the Kingdom would suddenly invade life "from above" in a cataclysmic act in which God, or he himself as God's agent, would overthrow the existing evil society and establish a new age of light and life.[8]

[7] Quoted by C. W. F. Smith in IDB, III, 156.
[8] Cf. Albert Schweitzer, *Quest of the Historical Jesus* (New York: The Macmillan Co., 1948).

Others think of Jesus' understanding of the Kingdom as a society gradually growing within life as men increasingly pray for and perform God's holy will.[9] Still others assert that Jesus taught that the Kingdom had been realized already and that this fact would be made known in world judgment and renewal.[10] In addition, there are various combinations of these views.

Ernst Lohmeyer in his book *Our Father* interprets each petition of the prayer apocalyptically. He states: "The Lord's Prayer first has an apocalyptic basis, i.e., it is governed by a contrast of opposites, the tensions between the holy God and his world, and the evil one and his world." [11] The prayer, though offered today, looks to the eschatological future for its final fulfillment. The present, however, is not without God's blessing. Today's bread is from God; the Christian community of the present is also God's own creation in Christ. Contrary to most apocalyptic readings of events, the Lord's Prayer sees the present order as not destroyed but renewed. Also, apocalyptic imagery is missing from the prayer.

Again it should be said that unless an interpreter of the Gospels had on other grounds concluded that Jesus had an apocalyptist's view of how the Kingdom was to come, there is nothing in the Lord's Prayer itself to suggest such a view. It is as nonapocalyptic in its phrase-

[9] Cf. Maurice Goguel, *The Life of Jesus* (New York: The Macmillan Co., 1944).

[10] Cf. Charles H. Dodd, *The Parables of the Kingdom* (New York: Scribners, 1936).

[11] Ernst Lohmeyer, *Our Father*, p. 278.

ology as any statement could be. Even Lohmeyer finds it necessary to note that the "today" of God's blessing which is present in its petitions, is lacking in the typical imagery of apocalyptic writings.

Just what would the difference be between the intent of an apocalyptic prayer and a nonapocalyptic prayer? Briefly the difference would be that in an apocalyptic prayer the petitions would be for a rupture in the on-going order of events with a sudden invasion or act of God that would destroy the old and inaugurate a new order of life and being. This is what the author of the book of Revelation had in mind when, at the close of a lengthy description of the cataclysmic overthrow of the old heaven and earth, he prayed *Maranatha* (Aramaic) which the translators read "Come, Lord Jesus" (22:20).

A nonapocalyptic petition for the coming of the King-dom would be a prayer for its advent in a gradual sense that would continue but renew the order of life now present in harmony with the will of God. By all odds the majority of Christians praying this prayer today have such an outlook as this in mind. Only in times of crisis when there is a feeling among some that the end of the world may be near would their petitions have an apoca-lyptic accent.

What Jesus Said

When we turn to the teachings of Jesus themselves we find both the apocalyptic and nonapocalyptic outlook present. It is seldom possible to tell whether the apocalyptic statements accurately represent Jesus' own view, or whether they reflect the thinking of the church which transmitted them and tended to be apocalyptic itself.[12]

The threefold apocalyptic portrayal of the end of the age and the coming of the Son of man (Matt. 24; Mark 13; Luke 21) may well contain some genuine words of Jesus but seems also to involve the thinking of the church, if not the actual adaptation of Jewish apocalyptic materials to Christian use.

Beside this, however, we must place words that describe the coming of the Kingdom through the process of growth and development. There is "first the blade, then the ear, then the full grain in the ear" (Mark 4:26-29). There is also the yeast that slowly causes the dough to rise (Luke 13:20-21).[13] We likewise have the assertion of Jesus that in his deeds the kingdom of God has already come upon them (Matt. 12:28). It was in their very midst or within them (Luke 17:20-21).

In the end, the answer to the question remains paradoxical. There is evidence for both points of view in the gospel tradition. From the standpoint of the place of prayer in the coming of the Kingdom, however, which is really what this petition in the Lord's Prayer is concerned

[11] Cf. B. Harvie Branscomb, *The Gospel of Mark* in "The Moffatt New Testament Commentary" (New York: Harper, 1937), pp. 231 ff.

[13] Note, however, Bornkamm's view, supported also by C. H. Dodd and J. Jeremias, that these references to growth are found in "contrast parables," and so the idea of natural development is ruled out. *Jesus of Nazareth*, pp. 71 ff.

with, we are assured that *whether present or future, gradual or sudden, apocalyptic or nonapocalyptic, the Kingdom is a cause about which men should pray.* Doing the will of God within the limits of man's ability alone cannot bring it to pass. It is ultimately the gift of God who must act to make it real. Therefore we shall continue to pray to him: "Thy kingdom come, thy will be done on earth as it is in heaven."

This act of praying for the coming of the Kingdom implies many things. It calls for becoming like a little child (Mark 10:15), putting one's talents to work (Matt. 25:14-30), watching for its coming (Mark 13:33-37), repenting unto baptism (Matt. 3:2; 4:17), seeking to be perfect as God is perfect (Matt. 5:48), and striving to enter it (Luke 13:24). How can one pray in the spirit of the Lord's Prayer and neglect any one of these?

Chapter VII

Our Daily Bread

The petition in the Lord's Prayer for daily bread brings us to the basic physical needs of man; he requires bread, even though he does not live by bread alone (Deut. 8:3). Just as from the cross Jesus cried out: "I thirst" (John 19:28), so here also the reality of man's bodily needs is signalized. That Jesus had more than material bread in mind is quite likely, but that he was also actually concerned with man's physical needs seems to be certain.

Jesus was not an ascetic who denied the demands of the body as a means of deepening the soul. In contrast to John the Baptist, whose disciples fasted often as the disciples of the Pharisees did, his followers ate and drank. They even called Jesus a glutton and a drunkard (Matt. 11:19), because he socialized normally in the daily round of living. He called himself a bridegroom to justify his actions. At weddings one is not supposed to fast (Luke 5:33-34). The petition for bread must be understood within this attitude toward life.

God the Provider

The Essenes of the Dead Sea community were ascetics in their eating practices, but they represented only one line of Jewish religious inheritance. Food was usually regarded as essential among the Hebrews. In fact, God was known as the giver of food to mankind and deliberately praised because of it. It is he who "satisfies him who is thirsty, and the hungry he fills with good things" (Ps. 107:9). Such generosity is an expression of his steadfast love (vs. 8).

This emphasis upon food is not to encourage an epicurean attitude of excessive indulgence. In fact, excess here was discouraged. Only "the food that is needful" was given (Prov. 30:8). Even in the account of the Garden of Eden when food was provided by God there was a proscription. They were told: "You may freely eat of every tree of the garden" (Gen. 2:16), with one exception; discipline and obedience to God were required since they were commanded not to eat of the tree of the knowledge of good and evil.

In the mealtime prayers of later Judaism the faithful

also thanked God for providing food: "Blessed art thou, O God, king of the universe, who feedest the whole world with thy goodness, with grace, with loving kindness and tender mercy." This loving kindness was related to food as the prayer continues: "Thou givest food to all flesh. . . . Through thy great goodness food hath never failed us. . . . Thou nourishest and sustainest all beings . . . and providest food for thy creatures whom thou hast created. Blessed art thou, O Lord, who givest food unto all."[1]

The Jews who first heard the Lord's Prayer would not have been surprised by the petition for daily bread. In fact, if it had been missing they would have regarded the prayer as incomplete. So deeply engrained was the practice of praying about food that Jesus' inclusion of this theme was thoroughly Hebraic.[2]

The Temptation and the Feeding of the Five Thousand

The thought of God as the provider of food had even become attached to the messianic hope of the Jews. Land flowing with milk and honey and wine and milk "without money and without price" (Isa. 55:1) were a part of the

---

[1] Berak, VII, 11 *a*, 35. Cf. the article by J. Jeremias, "The Lord's Prayer in Modern Research," *Expository Times*, Vol. LXXI, No. 5 (Feb. 1960).

[2] The ninth of the Eighteen Benedictions reads in part: "Bless this year unto us, O Lord our God, together with every kind of the produce thereof. . . ." (*The Authorized Daily Prayer Book.*)

nation's expectation from God. Later, in the first century A.D., the Apocalypse of Baruch spoke of a new age in which one vine would have a thousand branches, and every branch would bear a thousand clusters of grapes; each cluster would carry a thousand grapes, and every grape would produce a core of wine. This was hyperbole, of course, but it speaks of the hopes for abundance in the messianic age that God would initiate when the Messiah came.

It is against such a background that Jesus' temptation to turn stones into bread must be understood (Luke 4:3 ff.). Should he be a bread-giving Messiah? There has been a close assessment of the details of the record of the temptations of Jesus in the wilderness because of a conviction that the early church has overlaid it with messianic connotations. This was to be expected. That this experience meant much to Jesus personally seems certain. It is necessary also to know what the Christian community thought.[3] The early church's witness to the issues of the day is important too. And the church's conviction that the temptations had a messianic significance was deep-seated.

According to the account of the temptations, Jesus refused to turn stones into bread, to be a bread-giving Messiah, because there was more to life than eating and drinking. Bread is not the only or the deepest need of man. But it is a need, and God has been concerned to

[3] Cf. Günther Bornkamm, *Jesus of Nazareth*, p. 54.

meet it. Jesus would proclaim the gospel first, and bread would follow.

As Jesus' ministry continued there occurred an event that all four Gospels record—the feeding of the five thousand (Mark 6:31-44; Matt. 14:13-21; Luke 9:10-17; John 6:1-14). Usually the emphasis in reading these accounts is placed upon the multiplying of the loaves and fishes. This is understandable. But it is more important to note what Jesus had done. *He had fed the people. He had given them bread. He who had taught men to pray for bread had provided bread.*

The Gospels leave no doubt but that the authors believed that this was actual bread. The crowd had stayed all day to hear Jesus' preaching, so that they were pressed for time to go to the village and buy food. Hence Jesus provided it. But by feeding hungry people he was not substituting material necessities for spiritual ones.

The significant element here is lifted up by the author of the Gospel of John who refers to the fact that the Passover was at hand (6:4). The feeding of the five thousand was a foretaste of the eucharist which Jesus was to establish at the Last Supper. The offer of "the true bread from heaven" (vs. 32) is what had materialized—and in the future would occur whenever the Lord's Supper was observed.

Does God give bread? In John's Gospel Jesus answers: "For the bread of God is that which comes down from heaven, and gives life to the world" (vs. 33). *Jesus himself is the answer to the petition in the Lord's Prayer.*

He is the bread of life. Whoever comes to him "shall not hunger" (vs. 35). In Jesus the church found the answer.

Bread for the Poor

The high spiritual level of the interpretation in John's Gospel of the feeding of the five thousand should not blind us, however, to the moral character of Jesus' summons to his followers to care for the poor. They needed the spiritual food provided in the eucharist; they also needed the bread for daily living.

Luke's version of the beatitude "Blessed are you that hunger now, for you shall be satisfied" (6:21) looks to a supply of bread for the poor. Even though Matthew's version of this same statement reads "hunger and thirst for righteousness" (5:6), this Gospel is not unaware of Jesus' concern for those who are physically hungry. Matthew even gives us the parable of the Last Judgment where one group which was blessed of God was composed of those who had fed the hungry and by so doing had fed the Son of man (25:35, 40).

The early church also sought to care for the hungry in what was called "the daily distribution" (Acts 6:1). Another expression for this service was "to serve tables" (vs. 2). So time consuming and energy sapping was this activity that the apostles decided they should appoint special persons to care for it, thus freeing them to preach the word of God. This was possibly the beginning of the order of deacons when seven men were selected and

111

apostolic hands laid upon them to set them apart for their work (vs. 6).

The point in this discussion is that in the service to "those who hunger" we are helped to see what the petition "give us this day our daily bread" means. Jesus had taught its significance, and the early Christian community had undertaken to fulfill it. Here was their sphere of responsibility as the people of God. In one sense they were being used by God to answer the petition in the Lord's Prayer.

What Does "Daily" Mean?

The variations between Matthew and Luke in the form of this petition for daily bread are usually unnoticed by the casual reader. The translations in English do not make it clear, for instance, that Matthew uses the aorist tense *dos* for "give," while Luke employs the present imperative *didon*. Again, Matthew uses the adverb *semeron*, "this day," and Luke the prepositional phrase *to kath' hemeran*, "each day." The differences result from the tense of the verb; no great variation in meaning is involved.

The real problem here is that in Greek the word *epiousion* is used in connection with daily bread. In the New Testament it is found only in the Lord's Prayer. Not until the fifth century does it appear again in a kind of account or cook book where it refers to a day's ration. Jerome thought that he found a form of the word in the apocryphal Gospel of the Hebrews where he translates it "of the morrow." On this basis the meaning would be "today's portion for the morrow." In the RSV of both Matthew and Luke the words "daily bread" are used for *epiousion*, although in both cases the translators have added in a footnote the alternative reading "our bread for the morrow."

Through the centuries there have been numerous readings which are interesting and, at the same time, bear witness to the problem. Origen suggests two possibilities, i.e. "bread of substance" and "bread for the future," and in each case considers it as referring to the Logos. Cyril of Jerusalem emphasizes earthly bread with the eucharist in mind. Both Gregory of Nyssa and Chrysostom think of it as physical bread such as the body needs. Luther regards it as the giving of daily bread in connection with God's providential order of the world. In his *Catechism* he enlarged this to include "good friends, trusty neighbors, and the like."

Biblical translations of the early period similarly show variations of readings. The Old Syriac carries "lasting" for "daily"; the Peshitta has "for our needs," and the Vulgate for Matthew's version the word "supersubstantial." [4]

The Old Testament and Daily Bread

The Old Testament sheds some light upon this theme, for, after all, what is involved here is not simply a word

[4] A most thorough analysis of these variations with suggested reasons is found in Ernst Lohmeyer, *Our Father;* cf. pp. 141 ff.

study but an understanding of God's relation to men in regard to food. The wider question of divine care and providence is also at issue in this discussion. There is the account of God's providing manna to the Hebrews during their wilderness wanderings.[5] Their deprivations were great, and without divine intervention they would have perished. "Behold," he said, "I will rain bread from heaven for you; and the people shall go out and gather a day's portion every day" (Exod. 16:4). On the sixth day they were to gather twice as much to take care of the sabbath needs, since they were to do no labor on the seventh day of the week.

An interesting detail is that they were to gather only a day's supply at a time. If they hoarded it for the future, it would spoil. *God provided daily.* But there were two exceptions: The double portion collected on Friday would last through Saturday—the sabbath must be preserved; and they were told to take a jar and place an omer of manna in it for future generations as a sign of God's care for his people. Traditionally this portion was thought to have been placed in the ark which became a concrete mark of God's presence among the Hebrews (Heb. 9:4). In this same way the "daily bread" for which Christ urged his followers to pray with confidence of being

[5] Manna is described in Exodus: "It was like coriander seed, white, and the taste of it was like wafers made with honey" (16:31). Some have thought it to be the gummy fruit of the tamarisk tree that falls in that area even today and is used by the Arabs for food.

heard is reminiscent of the "daily manna" in the wilderness days. This bread was sometimes called "angels' bread" or "heavenly bread."

In Proverbs 30:8-9, in words characteristic of the Wisdom Literature, we read: "Feed me with the food that is needful for me," and with great frankness the prayer goes on: "lest I be full and deny thee, . . . or lest I be poor, and steal, and profane the name of my God." This is true realism. In rabbinic sayings the expression "food that is needful for me" or "food that is enough for me" is an explanatory phrase.[6] It is like Jesus' insistence that they gather up what was left over from the feeding of the five thousand "that nothing may be lost" (John 6:12). Just enough daily providence—this is the spirit of the passage.

E. F. Scott regards the word *epiousios* as possibly an Aramaic term for which there is not a Greek equivalent. Taking it literally it means: "Give us this day our bread for tomorrow." He recognizes that this is not typical of Jesus' view of providence, like "do not be anxious about tomorrow" (Matt. 6:34). Scott suggests that our Lord may have been thinking of the laborer who made wages in one day that were sufficient only for the next.

In spite of this, Scott supports the usual translation "daily bread" and says: "The rendering 'our daily bread' is an exceedingly happy one. It evades all the difficulties

[6] Cf. H. L. Strack and P. Billerbeck, *Kommentar zum Neuen Testament aus Talmud und Midrasch* (4 vols.; Munich, 1922-28), I, 420 ff.

and yet expresses the thought which was certainly in Jesus' mind. He permits us to ask from God those things which are needful to our earthly life, but only for what will be sufficient for the passing day. For the unknown future we must trust ourselves to God." [7]

Is the Petition Eschatological?

The question as to whether the petition for daily bread is eschatological, looking toward the end of the age, would not likely occur to the typical worshiper on Sunday morning, who uses the prayer as it appears in the liturgy. Even to raise this question would seem to be largely academic. But to one who considers Jesus' total outlook as being in eschatological terms, the petition for food must be interpreted in the light of his viewpoint as a whole, even when the prayer taken by itself seems in no sense to be contemplating the end of time.

Increasingly the tendency has been to interpret the Lord's Prayer in eschatological terms, for largely similar reasons to those singled out in our study of the petition: "Thy kingdom come." [8]

It seems then, that the petition for daily bread can be prayed eschatologically in the light of certain recorded sayings of Jesus; it can be prayed non-eschatologically in

[7] *The Lord's Prayer*, p. 99.

[8] Cf. the article by C. W. F. Smith on the *Lord's Prayer* in IDB, Vol. III. as well as Lohmeyer's *Our Father*, and Bornkamm's *Jesus of Nazareth*.

the light of other recorded sayings of Jesus. This may seem confusingly paradoxical, but the paradox remains rooted in the Gospel accounts themselves.

An eschatological reading of "daily bread" would stress the banquet of God in the coming Kingdom, as when Jesus said: "You may eat and drink at my table in my kingdom" (Luke 22:30). Yet in his own lifetime Jesus serves man immediately (Mark 10:45). As the disciples have fellowship with him daily, they are attending a wedding feast, for he is a bridegroom (Mark 2:19). He also feeds the hungry multitudes on the way to the Passover (Mark 6:32-44).

The solution of the paradox may be that even though men may eat the daily bread of God now, in the future when the Kingdom is revealed in its fullness, the splendor of the present will be surpassed. God's generosity knows no bounds; earth and time cannot contain it.

A Community Petition

The Lord's Prayer in Matthew's version begins with the address, "Our Father"; Luke has the single word "Father." The original can be translated either way. We have already found the significance of the word "our" in relation to the community and the liturgical character of the prayer to be an important element in its interpretation.

In the present petition for daily bread, both Matthew and Luke stress the group aspect of the prayer. Each

117

uses the words "us" and "our." Since it is highly probable that the separate versions came down to the church through different literary channels, their agreement here is significant, particularly in regard to Luke who omits the word "our" in the opening address.

Who is intended by the "us" and "our"? Is anyone left out, not included? The Old Testament usually tends to limit such a reference to the nation of Israel, to God's people of the Covenant (cf. Isa. 43:20-21). There are exceptions to this, however, in the psalms and prophets where a universalism sometimes comes to the fore. Such is the case in psalm 145: "The eyes *of all* look to thee, and thou givest *them* [all] their food in due season. . . . Thou satisfiest the desire *of every living thing*" (vss. 15-16). This same universal offer of his gifts is implied in Second Isaiah: "Turn to me and be saved, *all the ends of the earth!* For I am God, and there is no other" (Isa. 45:22). He is the only source of supply for mankind. All must depend upon him.

In the Lord's Prayer the "us" and "our" are sometimes said to refer only to the eschatological community who one day will eat bread at Christ's table in the Kingdom that is to come. It is difficult, however, to limit the gifts of God to these alone, in the light of Jesus' offer of salvation to all. He called all who were weak and heavy-laden to come to him for rest. Would he not likewise bid all to pray for and receive daily bread?

We are on sounder ground when we regard the use of the words "us" and "our" in the prayer as due to the

118

fact that the community was to use it perhaps liturgically in worship. And even when an individual prayed the prayer, as many must have done and now do both in the church and out of it, he would be conscious of belonging to God's family.

Chapter VIII

Forgive Us Our Debts

In divine-human relations, as in human relations also, forgiveness is the great restorative. Without it the brokenness of relationships cannot be mended. It not only puts life together again but also releases a new spirit or energy into personal relations that is creative. The saying "to err is human but to forgive is divine" is a reflection of this fact.

A prayer without the petition "forgive us our debts" would be inadequate to meet the demands of daily living. Remove it from our experience, both in reference to God and to man, and all moral meaning would be lost from life. The words "forgive me," just as "forgive us," enable us to take up the struggle of living once again and move forward.

All Men Are Sinners

Behind this petition for forgiveness lies the conviction that all men are sinners. Paul's statement, "all have sinned and fall short of the glory of God" (Rom. 3:23), realistically reports an experience. If one were to disregard the words "sin," "sinning," and "sinners" in the Bible, it would no longer make sense.

Both the Old and New Testaments are concerned with the fact of sin, what sin does to personal relationships, how it comes between man and God, and the need for forgiveness. Its multiple references to the judgment of God, as well as its constant offer of the forgiveness of God, must be interpreted against the background of its insistence on the reality of sin. A society that considers sin as only a psychological maladjustment or a sociological aberration will not understand the Bible. Its message will seem superfluous from beginning to end.

It is no accident that after the creation stories in the first two chapters of Genesis the narrative of the Garden of Eden should immediately follow. The whole of the Bible is built upon these themes, *creation, sin,* and *redemption,* and forgiveness lies at the heart of what it has to say about the last of them.

This is not the place to examine all that the Scriptures have to say about redemption. We are concerned with a single and exceedingly brief petition at the heart of the

121

Lord's Prayer: "And forgive us our debts, as we also have forgiven our debtors" (Matt. 6:12), with Luke's variant: "And forgive us our sins, for we ourselves forgive every one who is indebted to us" (11:4).

Approaches to Forgiveness

In the Old Testament there are two main approaches to forgiveness, the cultic and what I have chosen to call the prophetic. In the first instance sacrifices and ritual were predominant; in the second a change of heart and repentance only were central. Many of the psalms reflect the prophetic approach.

The cultic point of view called for sacrifices and a ritual of atonement (Lev. 4:13 ff.; 6:2-7; Num. 15:22 ff.). Restitution was also required in this approach. Prayer and song sometimes accompanied the sacrifices (Ps. 20:3). The Day of Atonement was the culmination of Old Testament sacrifices and came on the tenth day of Tishri, the seventh month. Its ceremonies included offerings, sacrifices, cleansings, the slaying of a goat, and the driving of another upon which rested the sins of the people into the wilderness. During the period of the New Testament the goat was driven over a cliff in the wilderness in an area about twelve miles from the Holy City.[1]

---

[1] Cf. also the Holiness Code found in Lev. 17-26, and the Deuteronomic Code found in Deut. 12-26. Here proscriptions against ceremonially unclean practices and purification rites are given in detail.

These rituals were practiced in the time of Jesus. Those who first heard the petition "Forgive us our debts" would inevitably think of them; some might even wonder if Jesus had these in mind. What they meant to him personally and the extent to which he may have entered into them is not recorded. In one reference, however, he recalled Hosea's statement: "I desire mercy, and not sacrifice," and added: "For I came not to call the righteous, but sinners" (Matt. 9:13). In another instance he said to the Pharisees: "Something greater than the temple is here" (Matt. 12:6). His general teachings do not mention rituals. Yet he once cleansed the Temple.

At the same time that the elaborate rituals and sacrificial offerings were taking place, there was a prophetic approach to forgiveness that represented a reaction against the ceremonial in favor of simple repentance. The sacrifices and offerings had in some cases become a substitute for righteous living and justice in human relations. This was the situation when Amos represented God as saying: "I hate, I despise your feasts, and I take no delight in your solemn assemblies. Even though you offer me your burnt offerings and cereal offerings, I will not accept them, and the peace offerings of your fatted beasts I will not look upon" (5:21-22).

In this same vein Isaiah spoke for God, crying out: "What to me is the multitude of your sacrifices? says the Lord; I have had enough of burnt offerings of rams and the fat of fed beasts; I do not delight in the blood of bulls, or of lambs, or of he-goats" (1:11).

In place of these, Isaiah presented God's summons:

123

"Come now, let us reason together, says the Lord: though your sins are like scarlet, they shall be as white as snow; though they are red like crimson, they shall become like wool" (1:18).

Then the prophet added: "If you are willing and obedient, you shall eat the good of the land . . ." (vs. 19), thus reasserting the primacy of inner attitude and of outward obedience in the moral area of forgiveness.

The psalmists speak eloquently in this area also. God forgives *all* of man's iniquities (Ps. 103:3). He removes his transgressions from him as far as the east is from the west because he "pities his children . . . [and] remembers that we are dust" (vss. 12-14). He is also "gracious and merciful, slow to anger and abounding in steadfast love" (Ps. 145:8). One psalmist wrote: "I acknowledged my sin to thee [God] . . . I said, 'I will confess my transgressions to the Lord'; then thou didst forgive the guilt of my sin" (Ps. 32:5). Here is a direct approach to God in seeking forgiveness that disregards priestly rituals.

While there is little in the teachings of Jesus to suggest that he stressed the cultic and ritualistic, there is much to indicate that the prophetic attitude represented his basic approach to forgiveness. It is within this area of meaning, therefore, that the reference to forgiveness in the Lord's Prayer is best interpreted.

Debts—Sins—Trespasses

Are we to ask for the forgiveness of debts, sins, or trespasses? Actually there is little difference in their

124

meanings for the prayer. The words may be used almost interchangeably.

Matthew's use of "debts" is probably most Hebraic because a sin was considered a debt owed to God among the Jews. In Aramaic, the word is also related to a commercial term. Possibly for this reason it was translated by Luke into "sins," so that Gentiles would understand better. In addition Luke, after using "sins," adds "for we ourselves forgive every one who is indebted to us." The word "trespasses" which is found in some liturgies of the Lord's Prayer comes from Matthew 6:14 where reference is made to our forgiving men their "trespasses," and also to God's forgiving us our "trespasses."

Some interpreters find a deeper meaning in "debts" than in "sins." They regard it as a more inclusive term involving what man has done or must do with the gift of life as a whole, a gift which has placed him in debt to God. Sin, on the other hand, is considered as referring to an individual act or to acts of disobedience by which a man deviates from the will of God.[2]

Such fine distinctions may or may not have been in Jesus' mind when he gave the prayer. Nowhere in his teaching does he define sin in so many words. Essentially it is a breach of love, since for him love toward God and man constituted the Great Commandment (Matt. 22:37-40).

The Lord's Prayer itself offers no specific theological explanation of sin, such as the doctrine of original sin

[2] Cf. Lohmeyer, *Our Father*, pp. 168 ff.

125

does. Neither does it contain a prescribed course of action, such as offerings for atonement in order to experience forgiveness. Nor is here what Christians refer to as the atoning death of Christ for sin, except, as R. H. Mackintosh used to say, that it was Jesus Christ the Redeemer himself who gave the prayer, he who would die on the cross as the cost of forgiveness, God's forgiveness through him. Theological doctrines are implied; they are not openly present in the Lord's Prayer.

Jesus' Teaching Concerning Forgiveness

We must therefore turn to Jesus' teachings concerning the forgiveness of sin if we are to learn what he meant when he taught his followers to pray: "Forgive us our sins." He alone can guide us to the inner meaning of the prayer. Of necessity we must keep in mind the Hebraic background of the prayer, but to interpret it in the light of the Old Testament alone and neglect the viewpoint of its originator would be unsound. Jesus gave it and, in my judgment, prayed it himself in his own way. How would he have us decipher its petitions? It is he who has the key to unlock its divine mysteries.

First of all he insisted that a man should forgive his fellowmen, even to the point of showing love toward his enemies who abuse him (Matt. 18:21-22). How often should he be willing to do this? The teaching of the rabbis regarded forgiving three times as sufficient. Jose ben Jehuda said: "If a man commits an offence once they forgive him, a second time they forgive him, a third time they forgive him, the fourth time they do not forgive him." [3]

In the Manual of Discipline the Dead Sea covenanters are called upon to extend forgiveness *within the brotherhood*. How far this attitude should be extended to outsiders is uncertain. Proselytes who have joined the group, however, are included. The injunction to forgive reads: "They are to extend forgiveness to all among the priesthood that have freely enlisted in the cause of holiness, and to all among the laity that have done so in the cause of truth, and likewise to all that have associated themselves with them [i.e. proselytes]." [4]

In contrast to this, Jesus placed no, or possibly only one, limitation upon forgiveness. When Peter asked how often he should forgive one who sinned against him, Jesus replied: "I do not say to you seven times, but seventy times seven" (Matt. 18:21-22). The usual prescribed number of times among the Jews was seven. "Seventy times seven" suggests an infinite number. [5]

Conditional Forgiveness

The necessity to forgive others, however, if one is to be forgiven himself is made particularly clear by Matthew

[3] Cf. the Babylonian Talmud, Yoma 86*b*, 87*a*.

[4] *The Dead Sea Scriptures*, p. 47.

[5] In Luke the reply reads: "If he [your brother] sins against you seven times in the day, and turns to you seven times, and says, 'I repent,' you must forgive him." Compare Gen. 4:24 with Luke 17:3-4.

who has Jesus say, immediately following the Lord's Prayer: "For if you forgive men their trespasses, your heavenly Father also will forgive you; but if you do not forgive men their trespasses, neither will your Father forgive your trespasses" (6:14-15).[6]

This condition had been hinted at within the prayer itself, but not explicitly stated. In Luke the prayer reads: "For we ourselves forgive everyone who is indebted to us" (11:4), while in Matthew it says: "As we also have forgiven our debtors" (6:12). The Aramaic which probably lies behind Matthew's version makes little distinction between the past and present tenses, so the fact that Luke's version of this statement is in the present and Matthew's in the past may not be significant.

It would seem, in any case, that there is this single condition in the plea for forgiveness. Only one who has a forgiving spirit himself can ask expectantly for God's forgiveness. We should not view this condition legalistically, however, so as to conclude that we will be forgiven only to the extent that we have forgiven others. And yet our attitude toward forgiving others cannot be ignored in the prayer. In a tradition that Matthew carries in the Sermon on the Mount, Jesus said: "So if you are offering your gift at the altar, and there remember that your brother has something against you, leave your gift there before the altar and go; *first be reconciled to your brother*

[6] Note the Jewish parallel from Rabbi Judah (c. A.D. 90): In the name of Rabbi Gamaliel, he wrote: "As often as you are merciful, the All-Merciful will have mercy upon you"; cf. Tos. Baba Kamma IX, 30.

and then come and offer your gift" (5:23-24). In this case one is to interrupt his prayer in order to get his brother to forgive him. Forgiveness is always the greater part of reconciliation.

There is yet another situation to which Jesus referred that involves the spirit as well as the act of forgiveness. It is found in the parable of the Unforgiving Servant (Matt. 18:23-35). We are given here the story of a man who owed a large debt. The figure was ten thousand talents which would come to about ten million dollars. Jesus probably deliberately made the amount excessive in order to dramatize the point. When the man could not pay he was about to be sold into slavery along with his wife and children.[7] His plea for mercy, however, led his creditor to forgive him the debt.

In contrast to such considerate treatment, the debtor refused to forgive a fellow servant who owed him only a hundred denarii which was about twenty dollars. The original debtor who would not forgive the small debt was reported to his lord and forthwith cast into prison because he had refused to be merciful. The parable closes with the comment: "So also my heavenly Father will do to every one of you, if you do not forgive your brother from your heart" (vs. 35). Forgiveness is, therefore, both a responsibility on our part and an act of grace on God's. The Lord's Prayer would not have us forget this.

---

[7] Cf. Adolf Deissmann, *Light from the Ancient East,* trans. L. R. M. Strachan (Grand Rapids: Baker Book House, 1966). The author gives examples from papyri of imprisoning men because of debts.

Further Teachings of Jesus on Forgiveness

When we are asked to pray: "Forgive us our debts," we are encouraged to lift hopefully this petition before God as we remember three of Jesus' parables (Luke 15), those of the Lost Sheep, the Lost Coin, and the Lost Sons (The Prodigal Son). Here God is the shepherd who goes to look for the lost sheep *until he finds it*. Here God is the woman who sweeps the house over and over to locate the lost coin *until she finds it*. And God is also the father of the lost sons, one the prodigal away from home and the other the elder brother at home. He waits for his erring son to return, restores him to the family circle, and also asserts his love for the brother who stayed at home.

Manifestly the sheep and the coin could not repent, but the son who had indulged "in loose living" was moved to repent and cry out: "Father, I have sinned against heaven and before you; I am no longer worthy to be called your son" (vss. 18-19). Almost as though he had interrupted (we are not heard by God for our much speaking!), the father ordered a robe, ring, and shoes for his son and gave instructions for the preparation of a banquet with merry-making. His son who had been "lost" was now "found."

All three of these parables teach that God is desperately eager to forgive his children when they turn about and in repentance respond to his love. Commenting on the prodigal, Bultmann notes that the youth says only " 'Father, I have sinned against heaven and before you; I am no longer worthy to be called your son'—and then the fatherly kindness embraces him." He also points to the fact that the publican only needed to pray: "God be merciful to me a sinner" (Luke 18:9-14).[8] There was no call for extended penitential prayers so characteristic of Judaism before God would forgive.

Other instances could be cited to bear out the fact that God was always ready to forgive when the spirit of repentance was present. The sinful woman who interrupted the meal at the home of Simon the Pharisee to wet Jesus' feet with her tears, to wipe them with her hair, then to kiss his feet and anoint them with ointment —this woman was forgiven and in return showered him with love (Luke 7:36-50). The paralytic whose friends had brought him to Jesus with considerable effort as they let down his bed through the tiles of the roof was likewise told that his sins had been forgiven (Luke 5:17-26).

There is yet another revealing situation that has bearing upon forgiveness as Jesus understood it and therefore helps to illuminate the petition for forgiveness in the Lord's Prayer. While he hung on the cross, looking down to the religious leaders who had sought his death, to the people who had blindly accepted an authoritarian religion, and to the soldiers who were carrying out a cruel order, Jesus said: "Father, forgive them; for they know not what they do" (Luke 23:34). Did he detect any spirit of repentance in these persons? Was he excusing them because of their ignorance? Such amazing love

[8] *Theology of the New Testament,* I, 24.

under such circumstances casts a warmth and splendor upon everything that Jesus had taught concerning forgiveness.

Forgiveness When?

The forgiveness we need and the forgiveness we seek is for today. The aorist tense of the verb *aphiemi*—forgive—which both Matthew and Luke employ, carries this sense of immediacy. Who can put off being forgiven? It is an existential need and an existential experience.

Those who consider the prayer as eschatological regard the petition as referring to forgiveness also at the end of the age. The last judgment of man is the time of God's visitation and final forgiveness. This does not mean that the forgiveness of the present time is not real or permanent, but that at the "last day" (John 11:24) God's evaluation of man's life will be finalized.

Modern man, in spite of the bomb, does not realize the extent to which the Christian community lived in anticipation of the end of time. It was a glorious expectation, for here the woes of life would be done away and the evils of existence conquered. But it was also a frightening anticipation, for men would meet God "face to face." Forgiveness under such circumstances would be of ultimate significance. It would be the difference between life and death.

In the meantime—the time of the now—men must daily pray for forgiveness, just as they must daily forgive others. E. F. Scott has noted that some regard the Lord's

Prayer as ingrown; it invites us, they say, to think only of ourselves. But in this petition, that is not the case. We also forgive and have forgiven our debtors. Even our own forgiveness is conditioned by this fact. In forgiving others we break the shell of selfishness. As Scott says: "All that Jesus teaches elsewhere of how we should act towards others is summed up and brought to a point in these few words, 'as we forgive those who trespass against us.'" He then adds significantly: "At the root of all our social problems lies the one sad fact that men are unforgiving." [9]

* *The Lord's Prayer*, p. 102.

Chapter IX

Lead Us Not into Temptation

Of all the petitions in the Lord's Prayer, the one against temptation is at the same time in some respects the most needful and the most problematical. It is particularly needful because all men experience temptation in one form or another and at one time or another. Here is a constant struggle for the Christian. The more spiritual he becomes the more refined and insidious are his temptations. A pull toward the grosser sins is not nearly so disarming as the drive in the direction of pride, compromise, and rationalization.

This petition is also the most problematical for its suggestion that God himself tempts men. How can this be? We remember the warning in the letter of James: "Let no one say when he is tempted, 'I am tempted by God'; for God cannot be tempted with evil and he himself tempts no one" (1:13). Is this statement a contradiction of the petition in the Lord's Prayer?

Sources of Temptation

The fact is that in the Bible the source of temptation is interpreted in three different ways. It is represented as coming from evil sources outside man, from evil desires within man, and also from God. Furthermore no attempt is made to correlate the three views. Experience here is greater than logic that would press for a simplified unitarian explanation.

Temptation from the Outside

In the account of Jesus' temptations in the wilderness the experience is related in such a way that the evil suggestions come to Jesus from the devil who challenges his messiahship as the Son of God (Matt. 4:1-11; Luke 4:1-13). In Mark the devil is called "Satan" (1:13). In Greek, "Satan" is considered a proper name; Aramaic does not so regard it. In any case, the tempter comes to Jesus as a personal figure apart from himself.[1] There is

---

[1] In another sense, however, God was behind this experience in the wilderness for it says that Jesus was "led by the Spirit" for this lonely vigil of forty days (Matt. 4:1; Luke 4:1). Mark says that "the Spirit immediately drove him out into the wilderness" (1:12).

even a conversation between them. It has been said that it is as though two rabbis were talking together.

The source of temptation in personal terms is reflected in the fact that several names are given to the devil. Those in Judaism included Azazel, Sammael, Beliar, and Mastema. In the New Testament the name Beelzebul is also used for the devil (Matt. 10:25). The KJV here has Beelzebub.[2]

Beelzebul is sometimes called "the prince of demons" (Matt. 12:24). He rules over a company of evil spirits or demons and was regarded as in control of the earth and mankind. This is but temporary, for Jesus' victory over him in the Temptations and later on the cross and by his resurrection has already broken his stranglehold, although the final victory is yet to become evident.

Another illustration of the view that temptation is due to evil sources outside man may be seen in Jesus' account of the evil spirit who was cast out of a house (i.e. a person). When he saw that the house was swept clean but remained unoccupied, he brought back "seven other spirits more evil than himself" who entered to dwell there (Matt. 12:43-45). The last state of the man was "worse that the first." [3]

More will be said later concerning the evil or the evil

[2] Beelzebub was used by Jerome in the Vulgate. It may have had its origin in the name Baalzebub. Cf. II Kings 1:2 where the god of Ekron is called Baalzebub, meaning "lord of flies."

[3] Cf. Rudolf Otto, *The Kingdom of God and the Son of Man*, trans. F. V. Filson and B. Lee-Woolf (Boston: Beacon Press, 1957), p. 97, for a reference to Beelzebul as "lord of the house."

one who is the source of temptation. Here it is sufficient to note that one line of biblical thought regards temptation as having its origin outside man.

Temptation from Within Man

A second view of the source of temptation in the Bible is that it comes from within man himself. The statement in James against holding God responsible for man's being tempted goes on: "Each person is tempted when he is *lured and enticed by his own desire.* Then desire when it has conceived gives birth to sin; and sin when it is full-grown brings forth death" (1:14-15).

John's Gospel also refers to the internal source of evil or temptation in man when it notes that light came into the world (through the advent of Jesus) but that "men loved darkness rather than light" (3:19). There is no further analysis in terms of such ideas as the carnal heart or original sin to explain why men loved darkness. It does, however, say that those who loved darkness did so "because their deeds were evil." Doing evil they continued to love evil or could not break from its grasp.

In yet another reference Jesus criticizes the Pharisees who were meticulously careful to keep the laws against uncleanness, who cleansed "the outside of the cup and of the dish." Inside, however, they were "full of extortion and wickedness" (Luke 11:37-41). Here it is made clear that the source of evil is an inner reality. In this same vein Jesus said that the Pharisees were like whitewashed tombs, which were bright and beautiful outside, but within they were full of dead men's bones. These religious leaders outwardly gave the appearance of being righteous, but *within* they were "full of hypocrisy and iniquity" (Matt. 23:27-28).

The inwardness of evil was stressed also by the author of psalm 51. He prayed that God would give him a clean heart and teach him wisdom *in his secret heart* and put a right spirit within him, because he experienced the inner pull, from the heart, toward evil.

Temptation from God

The third interpretation of the source of temptation which we meet in the Scriptures and other Hebrew writings is that it is sent upon man by the deliberate act of God. He is seen as putting the Hebrews "to the test" through the centuries (Judith 8:25). Abraham, Isaac, and Jacob alike were tested and "tried with fire." The author of Judith says that "the Lord scourges those who draw near to him *in order to admonish them*" (vs. 27).

In the book of Job, God is a party to the temptations that come to this good man who suffers unbearably. He allows Satan to bring these miseries upon him in order to prove that Job was blameless and upright. Satan in this great drama of Wisdom Literature is not the devil of the New Testament, but a kind of prosecuting attorney who goes in and out of heaven accusing men before God.

The Temptations in the life of Jesus were referred to earlier as an example of the external character of temptation. The devil comes to Jesus from the outside. On the other hand it was noted that God caused Jesus to be tempted; the Holy Spirit led him into the wilderness for this very purpose. Here he meets the worst that can befall a man in the tempting hour as various procedures for his work as the Messiah, procedures that are contrary to God's will, are offered him. But he remains firm in his loyalty to God and overcomes the devil's hold upon the world. In the testing hour to which God introduced him, he won a victory.

Even though Jesus accomplished a mighty act in breaking the devil's grip upon men by holding firm in the hour of temptation, he was still to wrestle with the devil in the mission before him. Luke's account of this occasion closes with the words: "And when the devil had ended every temptation, he departed from him until an opportune time" (4:13).

Luke also notes that at the end of the earthly journey, when Jesus was speaking to his disciples during the Last Supper, he said to them: "You are those who have continued with me in my trials" (22:28). The word translated "trials" here is *peirasmos* which has the meaning of putting one to the test or of being tempted. And sometimes it is God who puts men to the test in order to serve his divine purpose through them.

It is in this light that the author of Hebrews views Jesus' temptations. They were to prepare him for the office of the great high priest and to make expiation for the sins of the people. In bold and outspoken tones he writes: "For because he [Jesus] himself has suffered and been tempted, he is able to help those who are tempted"

139

(2:18). This has been referred to as "atonement by sympathy." [4] The point here is that the temptations Jesus faced and overcame were used by God, actually sent by God, to prepare Jesus to fulfill his calling.

The book of Psalms also reflects the view that God tests men: "The Lord tests the righteous and the wicked" (Ps. 11:5). And Lohmeyer quotes a Midrash on psalm 60:4 which says "Thou hast set up a banner for those who fear thee (banner in the Midrash is interpreted once as temptation) that they may be raised up for the sake of righteousness." [5] Again the purpose of such temptations is to deepen and enrich the one being tempted and to fulfill God's purpose. It is good, therefore, and not evil.

"Lead Us Not"

In the light of the three approaches to temptation that we have been considering the petition:

> "And lead us not into temptation,
>   But deliver us from evil" (Matt. 6:13)

takes on a new meaning. The idea that God sometimes leads men into temptation for their benefit and for realizing his own purpose with them, as in the case of Jesus, helps us to understand the petition. Why, then, should Jesus urge men to pray against it?

[4] T. H. Robinson, *The Epistle to the Hebrews* (Naperville: Allenson, 1933), p. 50.

[5] Lohmeyer, *Our Father*, p. 201. Cf. Billerbeck, I. 135: Gen. R. 55 fol. 34 *d*.

But were they actually being told in the Lord's Prayer to pray against this kind of temptation? Might not Jesus have had in mind the temptation that stems from outside sources, from the devil and his evil host? Is it not also possible that he was thinking of the temptations that come from evil desires within man?

If these were in Jesus' mind when he gave this petition he would be inviting men to pray that they would not be caught in a temptation that would be too much for them to meet. Later he was to say to the disciples in the Garden of Gethsemane: "Watch and pray that you may not enter into temptation; the spirit indeed is willing, but the flesh is weak" (Matt. 26:41). Because of the weakness of the flesh they would need God's constant help in the area of temptation.

The morning and evening prayers of the Jews, which may have been written as early as the first century B.C., are in this same vein. Such words as "Set my portion in thy law and accustom me to the performance of religious duties . . . and lead me not into sin, or into iniquity, or into temptation, or into contempt" [6] constitute a prayer for support in the hour of trial.

Rabbinic religion frequently went beyond the Old Testament. In regard to temptation, for instance, the rabbis held to a variety of views concerning goodness. Claude Montefiore points this out in relation to temptation: "If you can resist temptation many times successfully, you may be regarded as immune for ever; or, on the

---

[6] Berak, 60 b.

141

other hand, *you are never safe from the snares of* (especially sexual) *temptation."* [7] Therefore there was always the need for God's help. Is not this what Jesus had in mind in the petition of the Lord's Prayer against temptation?

Even in situations where temptations are regarded as sent by God, however, the petition may be that God would give strength to his children while he himself was testing them. May they pass through the hour of trial by his grace, to his glory, and to the deepening of their own lives! As psalm 34 says: "The Lord redeems the life of his servants; none of those who take refuge in him [in the hour of trial?] will be condemned" (vs. 22). Supporting the faithful in the time of temptation is a part of God's redemption itself.

The book of Revelation envisions the church as passing through a period of deep struggle in which it will be tempted to lose heart and soul as God moves within history to bring time to an end. It is the eschatological period of woes. The Christians are not to be delivered from the holocaust; they are to overcome or conquer even in the face of martyrdom (Rev. 2:7, 11, 17, 26; 3:5, 12). But God will guard them and grant them, if they remain faithful in Christ, final victory (12:4-6, 13-16). At such a time the petition "Lead us not into temptation" will be needed.

[7] C. J. G. Montefiore and H. M. J. Loewe, *A Rabbinic Anthology* (New York: The World Publishing Company [Meridian Books], 1960), pp. 34-35.

Deliverance from Evil

The words "Deliver us from evil" are sometimes regarded as a separate petition. But they may also be considered as an explication of the words, "Lead us not into temptation," similar to the petition: "Thy kingdom come" which is followed by: "Thy will be done on earth as it is in heaven." In both cases we have, in my opinion, an example of parallelism often found in Hebrew poetry.

E. F. Scott suggests that in Luke, where the petition against temptation is not followed by the prayer for deliverance from evil, the author felt the latter to be redundant, repetitive of what had just preceded it. Yet, Scott concludes that it is a separate petition and asks: "We have prayed not to fall into temptation, but what if we have already fallen? . . . The last petition, so far from being superfluous, may be regarded as the emphatic one. . . . We pray to God because there is evil within us and all around us, and we can do nothing without his help." [8]

Sometimes it is held that the words "Deliver us from evil" are broader and more inclusive in their outreach. While the petition against temptation is focussed against moral and spiritual struggles of life, this one is directed toward the physical and social confrontations with evil. Was this not the reason Jesus healed, gave hope to the poor, and ministered to the outcasts? Surely these situations do give rise to temptations and Jesus was acutely sensitive to this fact. But is not all temptation

[8] *The Lord's Prayer,* p. 107.

basically a moral and spiritual matter? When material struggles prove to be greater than we can carry, we are tempted to lose faith, and then the temptation is more than a physical and social matter. It is of the heart and soul.

To be delivered from evil means in either case, however, that men shall not be overwhelmed in the tempting hour. May they not be found in a situation beyond their power to handle, or if so, may they count upon God's power and support to deliver them, enabling them to overcome. Paul's assurance that God's faithfulness will see to it that men will not be called upon to bear impossible burdens supports this view: "No temptation has overtaken you that is not common to man. God is faithful, and he will not let you be tempted beyond your strength, but with the temptation will also provide the way of escape, that you may be able to endure it" (I Cor. 10:13).

From Evil or the Evil One

Those who are familiar with recent versions of the Bible already know that an alternative reading for "from evil" is "from the evil one." [9] In Greek, the genitive *tou ponerou* is either neuter or masculine. If neuter, the translation is "from evil"; if masculine, it is "from the evil one."

"From evil" would be a general reference as in the Didache passage which reads "from all evil" (10:5).

[9] Cf. footnote in RSV.

"From the evil one" would suggest a personal source of evil. This is regarded by some as being more eschatological, referring mostly to the final testing hour. The evil one would be the devil or other representations of the source of evil in personal terms.[10]

In the book of Revelation various meanings of the evil one are combined in the figure of the dragon, as where the author explains the source of the struggles on earth just prior to the end: "The great dragon was thrown down [from heaven], that ancient serpent, who is called the Devil and Satan, the deceiver of the whole world—he was thrown down to the earth, and his angels were thrown down with him" (12:9). This would be "the evil one" referred to in the Lord's Prayer. He came down to earth and was "in great wrath, because he knows that his time is short!" (vs. 12.)

There need be no basic contradiction, however, between "from evil" and "from the evil one," except that the latter affirms a personal source of evil and may be more eschatologically oriented. It would bring to the mind of those who prayed visions of the apocalyptic expectation and imagery of the end of the age.

Again the word "us" appears in this petition, thus asserting that it is a prayer of the Christian community. While individuals may pray it meaningfully, the church must also offer it. She is the "body of Christ" and as such

---

[10] The Eastern Church since Origen has favored the masculine reading "the evil one," while the Western Church mostly urged the neuter "from evil." Both Augustine and Luther favored the latter.

needs to pray that she will not lose her identity through succumbing to temptations. Evil or the Evil One would destroy her and her witness. In the testing hour, whether it comes from the devil's challenge, from the egoistic desires of her members taken collectively, or from a trial sent by God—she must pray for deliverance and victory over it.

The Doxology

Although the doxology, "For thine is the kingdom and the power and the glory, forever. Amen," is probably not a part of the original prayer, its ideas are in harmony with biblical thought and the teachings of Jesus. The Didache contains it in a briefer form, reading: "Thine is the power and the glory" (8:2). It may have been used by the church responsively.[11] Again, it is possible that it was spoken as a part of the prayer itself to round it off and give it liturgical smoothness. The best of the earlier manuscripts, however, do not contain it.

Doxologies were typical in Hebrew prayer. Instances of their use abound in the psalms (Pss. 29:1; 118:29; 145:11-12). When David made his farewell prayer he said: "Thine, O Lord, is the greatness, and the power, and the glory, and the victory, and the majesty; . . . thine is the kingdom, O Lord, and thou art exalted as

---

[11] In the Didache 9–10 this would seem to be the case. There we find two responses of "Thine is the glory forever" (9:2-3; 10:2,4) and a third which reads: "for thine is the glory and the power through Jesus Christ forever" (9:4).

head above all" (I Chron. 29:11). The similarity of these words to those in the doxology of the Lord's Prayer raises the question whether the church did not actually take it from this source.

Both the expressions "for ever" and "amen" were also typically Hebrew. And they were likewise carried over into Christian thought and usage (Rom. 16:27; I Peter 4:11; 5:11; Rev. 1:6).

Paul's doxology at the close of a lengthy argument in which he sought to explain the refusal of the Jews to accept Jesus is particularly expressive and in harmony with the appendix to the Lord's Prayer:

> O the depth of the riches and wisdom and knowledge of God! How unsearchable are his judgments and how inscrutable his ways!
> "For who has known the mind of the Lord,
> or who has been his counselor?"
> "Or who has given a gift to him
> that he might be repaid?"
> For from him and through him and to him are all things. To him be glory forever. Amen.
>
> (Rom. 11:33-36.)

When we use the Lord's Prayer with the doxology we are thinking and feeling at the deepest and most profound level of Hebraic-Christian religion. New life in the kingdom of God through the power of God and unto the glory of God is the goal of creation and redemption.

Epilogue

The Lord's Prayer is a living, breathing, spiritual reality which quickens life with meaning, unites man and God, and gives a voice to the deepest longings of our hearts that otherwise might remain mute within us. It came out of the life of the Son as he held communion with the Father. It was not a study but a story of his relationship with God.

George A. Buttrick says in his book *So We Believe, So We Pray*: "Two signs of Jesus abide, though all else be ignored or forgotten—a prayer and a cross. People who are ignorant about the Bible can recite the Lord's

Prayer, and they know that Jesus was crucified. These are His memorial: not a tombstone or a moneyed foundation, but a simple prayer and a gallows set against the daybreak. About five hundred million people say the prayer. If they really prayed it, they could change the world." [1]

As I have intimated throughout this book, it is my conviction that the Lord's Prayer is the greatest single utterance of Jesus when interpreted within the circle of his own life and thought. It is alive with his dedication and faith in the heavenly Father; it is warm with love and trust; it is deep in its moral earnestness; it is bright with his belief in the coming of the Kingdom. In a very real sense it is a portrait of his mind and person. He both lived and prayed it. It was his very own prayer before he gave it to his disciples—and to us.

A Prayer for All

The Lord's Prayer can be used by anybody, anywhere. Its universal spirit makes it possible to appropriate it personally under all circumstances. No geographical, racial, social, economic, or political boundaries limit its pertinency.

Eva Alvey Richards in *Arctic Mood* gives a translation of the Lord's Prayer by Nasholook, Segavan, and Tooruk which they made together by the light of a kerosene lamp in a schoolhouse at Wainwright. It illus-

[1] George A. Buttrick, *So We Believe, So We Pray* (Nashville: Abingdon Press, 1951), p. 121.

trates how the prayer can be prayed in a diversity of situations with relevancy and realism:

Our God Father who is this time in His village, holy is that name. Your Kingdom Come. Please our Father, you do for this place the same like in your village. Sealmeat this day give us. Our many things we owe to people and village, we give the people. Send people many things good like that peoples is good the same, and from many bad days save every people. Amen.[2]

It is not the novelty of wording in this translation that is of greatest significance, but the fact that the prayer can have meaning in the arctic wastes, thousands of miles from Judean hills and nearly two thousand years distant from the time when Jesus gave it to his disciples. In this same vein, phrase by phrase, the Lord's Prayer can be applied to every person's situation and need. It is timely and timeless.

There is always occasion to hallow God's name, to look toward the Kingdom as God's will on earth in any given situation, to depend upon him for our physical needs, to turn to him for forgiveness, and to seek his strength in meeting the onslaught of evil.

When men feel deeply but do not know how to express their need in prayer, the Lord's Prayer is always at hand to be used personally. We may make it ours so that its phrases will carry the burden and joy of our hearts to the heavenly Father.

[2] Eva Alvey Richards, *Arctic Mood* (London: Caxton Publishing Company, 1949).

A Prayer for Liturgy

Of all prayers of the Christian tradition, none has been used more widely than the Lord's Prayer, referred to in Latin as the *Pater noster*. Not only before but also after the continental Reformation was this the case, and so it remains to this very day.

In Luther's Mass of 1526 prepared for Wittenberg, the Lord's Prayer was recited in paraphrase following the sermon. The two Catechisms, the "Long" and the "Short" of 1529, provided instruction on four topics: the Commandments, the Creed, the Lord's Prayer, and the Sacraments. At Strassburg the Mass was first celebrated in German during Holy Week of 1524. It included the Lord's Prayer with a *Libera nos* and *Agnus Dei*.

At Geneva in 1538 John Calvin set up the service, dividing the Decalogue in two. He placed the Lord's Prayer in paraphrase immediately after the intercessory paragraph. Zwingli at Zürich in 1523 also prepared a reformed version of the Mass. In this service, after the pastor invited the congregation "to the worthy celebration of the supper," the Lord's Prayer was said kneeling. The continued use of the Lord's Prayer in the Reformation on the continent shows how deeply it had become engrained in the liturgical expression of the clergy and people alike.

The same was true in England where the Book of Common Prayer in its various versions regularly reserved a place for the Lord's Prayer. The First Prayer Book of 1549 used it both in the morning and evening prayer services. The service of Baptism in the Second Prayer Book of 1661 called for the Lord's Prayer and a Thanksgiving at the close of the service. After 1662 the Doxology was attached to the Lord's Prayer. At the same time the prayer was added to the service of Confirmation.

A special word should be said concerning the double use of the Lord's Prayer in the morning prayer service of the Church of England. This is a reflection of the medieval practice of repeating the prayer in silence to prepare the soul for worship; now it is uttered aloud since the Reformers insisted that nothing should be private or secret in the church's worship. The second time the Lord's Prayer is used in the service is after the worshipers have heard the Word of God in Scripture and in the Creed. Now all join together through the use of this prayer to say: "Thy will be done."

The Eastern Orthodox Church likewise used the Lord's Prayer liturgically. It was said in Morning Prayers, Evening Prayers, in connection with the Order of Confession, and in preparation before Holy Communion and in Thanksgiving after Holy Communion.

John Wesley's Orders of Common Prayer of 1784 included the Lord's Prayer as "scriptural and rational." He advised the American churches to use it in connection with this service each Sunday, although he himself said it daily. He titled the service *Order for Morning Prayer, Every Lord's Day*. The prayer was placed following the prayer of absolution and was said by all. It was also used after the serving of the elements in the Communion service.

These few illustrations from the Reformation period and afterward indicate how deeply committed the church was to the formal use of the Lord's Prayer in worship. A broader liturgical review including present-day practices would take us too far afield but would show that it has an unparalleled place in the life of the church. Regular services of worship, baptisms, weddings, funerals, and all other communal meetings that involve a formal or even informal expression of our religious commitment to Christ are brought into spiritual focus by the use of the prayer which was his very own, given to us by him so that, in turn, it might also become our very own.

It has been said that the Lord's Prayer was one prayer that was certain of an affirmative answer, whether prayed in one's personal devotional life or said as a participant in corporate worship; its petitions could not help being within the will of God.

Index of Scripture References

Numbers in italic indicate references to footnotes

Index of Subjects

Numbers in italic indicate references to footnotes